THE RIVAL CITIES
Venice and Genoa

TRADE ROUTES SERIES
*Prepared under the general editorship
of Edward R. Sammis*

RIVAL CITIES
VENICE AND GENOA

by M. GREGG ROBINSON

McGRAW-HILL BOOK COMPANY
New York · Toronto · London · Sydney
St. Louis · San Francisco · Mexico · Panama

THE RIVAL CITIES

Library of Congress Catalog Card Number: 69-16259

1234567890   HDEC   754321069

To My Father
A Man Of Integrity

CONTENTS

People from the
mainland flee to the
islands to escape from
Attila.

An Island City

"Attila is coming!"

For the people huddled in the piazza of a little Italian village not far from the Adriatic Sea, the words of Guiseppe Rosinelli were like icicles of fear. The voice of the young man who had brought the news trembled, then rose.

"It is true! The Huns are sweeping toward our village. Attila himself is leading them."

Even those with the stoutest of hearts turned pale. The name of Attila was the name of terror itself. Older folk could remember the last time the barbarians had come swooping into Italy. But then they had been able to count on the Roman Legionnaires to drive them back. But now, on this pale autumn morning in the year 452 A.D., there were no Roman soldiers to stand between them and the invader—for Rome was no longer a great power.

Guiseppe's arms fell. He waited. He had run all night, not stopping for food or rest to bring this warning to his fellow townsmen. Now it was up to them to decide what to do.

Wordlessly each turned to his neighbor. Where shall we go? Where can we flee? What hope is there when Attila marches?

"The islands," murmured a fisherman, Daniele Cattaneo.

"Yes, the islands." The two words passed from mouth to mouth. Parallel to the coast a mile or so offshore lay a cluster of islands. They were little more than tufts of marsh grass, but they did offer a hiding place, a refuge.

As the next day dawned, people from the village and the surrounding countryside were frantically loading their belongings, first into carts, then into barges and small boats for the trip to the islands. And they were none too soon. Even as the last boats left the shore, runners brought word that Attila and his men had already been sighted. Only hours after the townspeople had safely put water between themselves and the barbarians, Attila and his horde entered their village.

On the shore Attila stood glowering seaward. Infuriated that his quarry had escaped him, he vowed to pursue them even into their island fastness. But the Huns were not a seagoing people and did not know how to build seaworthy vessels. The islanders, who had been spying on the preparations, took heart when they saw how clumsily the barbarians were going about their business.

Daniele, the fisherman, called his most seasoned comrades to his side. If they did not seize this moment of advantage and make the most of it, they would all be put to the sword.

"The sea is the place for a seaman to meet his death," he said, "not the land."

The fishermen waited until the unwieldy Hun boats were well out on the water. Then they rowed to the attack. In and out among the top-heavy craft they went, darting, ramming, retreating. The Huns were heavily

armed, and, in the excitement, they tended to crowd to one side of the boat. Many of their makeshift boats capsized, dropping them into the sea. Others simply came apart. Panic seized the invaders, and those who remained alive made their way back to land. Attila, enraged, ordered the empty village put to the torch.

Fishermen capsize the Huns' craft to save their families from death.

The townspeople looked on sadly as they saw their homes go up in flames. "But at least," they said to one another, "we are alive."

Several days later, when the citizens were convinced that Attila had left for good, they began to think about returning to the mainland. Again, Daniele spoke up.

"Why do you wish to go back?" he asked. "Attila has left us nothing but rubble. These islands have been good to us. There will most likely come a time when we will be attacked again. Let us stay here. Most of us live by the sea. Let us live in the sea as well."

For many years, with each successive wave of barbarian invaders, the tide of refugees from inland had advanced to the islands and then returned to their land homes. The Lombards in the sixth century were by far more ferocious than any barbarian tribe who had come before, fearsome as these had been. One Lombard chief, Alboin by name, had an enemy's skull made into a wine cup from which he drank to his memory.

These latest intruders differed from those that had come and gone before—they intended to stay. To the defenseless people in the small Italian towns, the islands in the salt marsh appeared more desirable than ever. Many refugees moved there. Gradually there arose a chain of twelve small townships scattered along sixty miles of coast.

Legend has it that the first of the new island dwellers offered up a prophetic prayer: "Now we kneel before a poor altar. But if our vows are not made to Thee in vain,

Attila led the Huns into Italy.

a hundred temples, O God, of gold and marble shall arise
to Thee." These twelve sandy islands were to become
the fabulous city of Venice.

Since the islands were little more than strips of mud
tufted with marsh grass, the settlers drove sturdy oak
pilings into the silt to raise their homes above the tides.
To reach the other islands, they plied the waters between
with small boats. So, from the very beginning, Venice
was distinctive for her method of building homes and as
a city served by canals instead of streets.

In 584, the twelve island townships combined and
established a headquarters on the Rialto, an island that
was to become famous as the hub of Venice's far-flung
trading activities. In 697, the townships elected their first
supreme magistrate, called the Doge. In the beginning
he was chosen by an assembly of all the people and, later
on, by a Grand Council, a kind of senatorial body. The
man for the job was picked because he had distinguished
himself as an outstanding citizen. He was elected for life
but was not allowed to make his office hereditary.

The community just coming into being would one day
take the form of what was to be known as a "city-
state"—a city so powerful that in some ways it was like
a nation, often controlling considerable surrounding terri-
tory and even some colonies across the seas. As a city-
state, Venice was to become more wealthy and more
famous than many a nation.

From the very beginning, the Venetians, with no large
land mass within their boundaries, made their living in one
way or another from the sea. They were fishermen; they
were sailors; they were traders in salt. By the middle
of the sixth century, their adventurous seamen in strongly

built ships were sailing down the Adriatic, across the Mediterranean, and putting in at ports along the Levant (what is now Syria, Lebanon, and Israel).

The port that showed the most promise for profit was Constantinople, capital of the flourishing Byzantine Empire. Founded by a colony of Greeks in 660 B.C., the city was called Byzantium until 324 A.D. Then, the Emperor Constantine, having brought together under his rule the two halves of the Roman Empire—western Roman Catholic and eastern Greek Orthodox—renamed the city Constantinople in honor of himself.

Constantinople, perched on the edge of a water link called the Bosporus connecting the Black Sea to the east with the Sea of Marmara, the Aegean Sea, and the Mediterranean Sea to the west, was strategically situated. Here, water routes and land routes converged. Goods coming by caravan and by ship from the east, south, and north were bought and sold here, then transported farther

Vatican fresco shows
Emperor Constantine
seated in the fore-
ground.

west to the ultimate consumer. Here merchants displayed their exotic wares: incense and myrrh from Arabia,
silks from far-off China, spices from the Indies, furs and
hides from the steppes of Russia.

Daily the quays were crowded with tiny dhows (native
sailing vessels) or large triremes (vessels propelled by three
banks of oars). Camels and ponies, dusty from a thousand
miles of travel and weighed down with bales of goods,
wound their way through the narrow streets.

The Venetian merchants saw clearly the possibilities for
commerce between the trading center of Constantinople
and lands to the west. With a race of skilled and hardy
seamen available to man her ships and shrewd merchants
to do her trading, Venice was soon to become the biggest
transporter and seller of such goods as silks, carpets,
incense, gold, and precious jewels to the still semibarbaric
people of Europe who yearned for such luxuries and who
were not only eager, but able to pay for them.

Emperor
Constantine

Pirates!

As time passed Venice's trade with the East increased. She became known as the "Queen of the Adriatic." But just when this trade was beginning to bring real prosperity, a new menace appeared to threaten the security of her overseas lifeline.

Across the Adriatic from Venice, the rock-girt harbors of the Dalmatian coast (now Yugoslavia) offered ideal hideouts for pirates. These sea-rovers, issuing forth heavily armed in their barques, began to prey on the richly laden merchant ships. Indeed, the corsairs proved so formidable that, by the ninth century, they were on the point of bringing Venice to her knees.

As the century came to a close, the buccaneers were growing ever more venturesome. They no longer even hesitated to prey on merchant vessels sailing in convoy (a group under guard). And the Venetian ships were not easy targets. They were built by the city to rigid specifications so that they could be converted in an instant from merchantmen to men-of-war.

When called upon, every man aboard—whether common seaman, clerk, merchant, or prince—was expected to fight. No one was exempt. The ships for which they fought were formidable vessels; they had stormed and

Early scene of Venice
from 13th century
book.

taken strongly-defended towns all the way to the
Bosporus. But the pirates were tougher. In the tenth
century, further emboldened by their successes, the
pirates sailed right up to the great lagoon at the edge of
Venice itself.

The pirates were ready to carry out their greatest coup
to date. From captured sailors they had heard about a
traditional Venetian ceremony that was held every year
on one of the outer islands, commemorating the refugees'
escape from the Lombards in the sixth century. Like the
mainlanders who built a new life on the islands, the
betrothed young women of Venice were taken to an island

A war galley of the 11th century could carry men or trading goods.

known as Castello, where a number of them would be married in a mass ceremony.

Just after nightfall two pirate ships dropped anchor on the seaward side of Castello. From each vessel the dark shadow of a longboat slid toward shore. The January night was cold. Members of the landing party shivered as they picked their way toward the ancient stone cathedral.

The pirate chief had his plan all worked out. The minute the brides-to-be reached the church where they were to await the arrival of their future husbands, his men would snatch them up and carry them off to their ships. (There was little chance of discovery since the bridegrooms' ship would stay at anchor on the opposite side of the island, the side nearest Venice.)

Each girl carried a small jeweled casket that contained her dowry. Not only would the pirates be able to sell the girls as slaves, but the hostages would have treasure and jewels as well! The pirate captain ordered his men into the underbrush.

Giggles and excited bits of conversation announced the arrival of the young girls. When the captain sounded a piercing whistle, the bushes came alive with shadowy forms. Muffled cries filled the night. The girls struggled, but they were helpless in the strong arms of the pirates. In no time the buccaneers had carried them down to their longboats.

As custom required, the grooms passed that same night waiting aboard ship until dawn. Nervous about their coming marriages, they paced back and forth on the deck of the Venetian ceremonial ship. The sun rose over the Adriatic, and the gaily decorated barge drew up to Castello. Leaping ashore, the young men scrambled up the hill. When they reached the church, they found it empty. The grounds were deserted.

One of the grooms bent down, then held his right hand aloft brandishing a jeweled sword and scabbard that one of the pirates had dropped as they dragged the women away.

"Pirates!" he yelled. "The girls have been kidnapped." The bridegrooms stared at each other in horror. Then they ran back to the ship and steered for Venice. They went directly to the palace of the Doge to report what had happened.

In theory, the power of the Doge was absolute. But in practice, authority varied with the man himself. The Doge did have unusual powers at his command, however, for he was not only the chief of all civic and military affairs, but of the local church as well.

The incumbent Doge was a man of strong character.

His face grew purple with rage as the couriers stammered out their news. He ordered a fleet made ready at once. The citizens of Venice shared the Doge's anger. Merchants offered not only their ships, but also their services. Fishermen and sailors volunteered.

Two days later, the Venetian vessels cleared the outer islands. It was a rough winter day. They were buffeted by the blustering gale. But, turning the situation to their advantage, the Venetians sailed before the wind for four days and five nights. As a result, they were never far behind their quarry. Sometimes, on the horizon they could glimpse the pirates' lateen sails. Meanwhile, the corsairs had decided to put into one of their nearest lairs—a small settlement where they hoped to get a good price for their female captives.

The Venetians were proceeding swiftly down the Dalmatian coast when they came on the pirate ships riding at anchor. Luck was with the pursuers. The buccaneers happened to be in the village carousing while the Venetian girls were being offered for sale on the auction block. The Venetians swarmed ashore and were already moving to the attack before their foes were even aware of their presence.

The pirates were taken off guard, away from their weapons and therefore unable to put up much of a fight. They were soon bound and led aboard the Venetian ships. The brides, rejoicing, were reunited with their husbands-to-be, and most of their dowery was recovered.

But the pirates were not to remain quiet for long just because of one defeat. Their continued activities cast a long shadow over Venice's chief source of income. So long as they lurked in their coves, ready to pounce, the

Venetians could never be certain that their shiploads of valuables leaving Constantinople would ever reach home port.

Doge Pietro Orseolo risked Venice's future to fight the pirates.

Just when Venice's fortunes had reached a critical low, the city elected a new Doge. His name was Pietro Orseolo. Like his predecessor, he was a man of great courage and spirit. But he was also more vigorous and aggressive; he was a man who would be willing to risk the republic's future on a single roll of the dice.

Orseolo, who was well-educated and came of a noble Venetian family, was elected Doge in 991. He had already amassed a considerable fortune and was known among his friends as an adventurous, but not a reckless man. The new Doge looked on life as a kind of athletic contest for which one must always be in training. As a part of his program of conditioning, he arose early every morning and exercised for forty minutes. In this way, he managed to keep his body strong and free of the paunch displayed by so many of his successful contemporaries. Rich though he was, Signor Orseolo was modest in dress and demeanor. He wore but one ring, an emerald given to him by his wife before they were married. His beard was neat and close-cropped, slightly streaked with gray; his nose was long and delicate; his eyes were penetrating.

The key to this man's distinction lay in his thoroughness as well as his courage. When he became Doge he approached the problems of his office with characteristic energy and enthusiasm. Doge Orseolo first accepted the premise that Venice was going down hill. Then he set out to discover the reasons for her decline. He emerged from a cloistered period of study convinced that, if the city-state was to become prosperous once more, she must expand. Most important, he concluded, was to increase her lucrative trade with Constantinople.

Unlike his advisers, Doge Orseolo was an optimist. He was determined that under his leadership Venice would once more become the Queen of the Adriatic, in fact as well as claim. Doge Orseolo determined to free Venice from the pirates once and for all. But he had patience enough to await a favorable moment.

He had a plan. For many years the pirates had been in the habit of demanding—and receiving—from successive Doges, an annual "tribute." This was in fact a bribe, in return for which they would agree not to rob Venetian ships—a promise which, of course, they never kept nor intended to keep.

When the pirates came to demand this tribute of the new Doge, Orseolo received them courteously and listened to their proposal as though he had never heard of the practice before. Then, explaining that it would take some time to lay hands on such a large sum, he promised to deliver the money in person at Lagosta, their capital, another harbor on the Dalmatian coast.

One morning the Doge's fleet appeared, as agreed, off Lagosta. At first the buccaneers were awed when they saw the huge flotilla. But the more they thought about it, the more they believed the size of the fleet was an indication that the Venetians were trying in this way to buy their safety and were willing to pay an enormous price for it.

Gathered at the seaward wall, watching as the Venetians approached, they joked about it among themselves.

"We'll take their ducats all right," chuckled one. "Then we'll go right on and take their ships, too."

At that moment the pirates saw something that filled them with consternation. One of their own vessels burst into flames. Then another, and another. Even as they watched, the Doge's ships were sailing through the fiery wreckage toward the walls of their city.

Before the pirates could decide what to do, they heard shouts at the northern gate of the city. Suddenly Venetians seemed to be all around them. Orseolo had secretly put a considerable force ashore the previous night.

The pirates ran for their arms, but they were too late. More Venetians even then were pouring into the city. Rattled, confused, and paralyzed by fear, the buccaneers

Doge Pietro Orseolo I
leaves the throne.

turned back toward the seaward ramparts. But here also
they were too late. In their aimless rushing to and fro,
they had given the Doge's men time to scale the undefended walls.

The pirates, when they discovered they were sur-
rounded, lost heart and quickly surrendered. Pietro
Orseolo's surprise had been an overwhelming success.
Having reduced the city to rubble, he sailed home again.
He could permit himself a satisfied smile as he thought
of all the mischief-makers of the pirate world safely below
decks in chains.

Thus Orseolo, in a single brilliant gamble, risking the
safety of his entire fleet, put an end to one source of
danger on the high seas.

Constantinople, source of such great riches, was once more accessible. No longer need Venetian ships go in convoy; they could travel unescorted.

Doge Orseolo II settles a dispute between Istria and Dalmatia.

The Shaping of a Financial War

While the Venetians had been kept busy in the Adriatic, the merchants of Genoa had found their way to Constantinople. Here the two rivals were to meet and eventually to clash.

In the beginning it appeared that the Venetians had little to worry about. They had been doing business with the Greeks for a long, long time. In the first quarter of the eighth century they had formed an alliance with Byzantium. The relationship was strengthened again by a new agreement arranged by Pietro Orseolo II in 1091. The Genoese were newcomers; their trade arrangements were not nearly so favorable as those enjoyed by the Venetians. For example, the Genoese had to pay a heavy tax on all goods traded in any of the ports of Byzantium. The Venetians traded tax-free. An even more favorable trade agreement was negotiated in 1095 after their fleet had helped to transport the Emperor of Byzantium and his troops to conquer the Greek islands. The Venetians were accustomed to receiving favors that the Genoese could not hope to have.

The merchants of Genoa had, so to speak, been able to get a foot in the door during the years when the Venetians were preoccupied with pirate harassment. The

Ancient map showing Corsica, Sardinia, Sicily, Italy, and Dalmatia.

pirates pretty much confined their activities to the Adriatic, while the Genoese, unlike the Venetians, could sail all the way home around the Italian boot in waters free from marauding ships. This gave them the advantage of being able to deliver goods bound for Europe to their home port in safety—a condition much appreciated by Constantinople merchants. From this time on the rivalry between the two cities began to grow on more equal terms. As the years passed, this competition intensified, until at last, during the fourteenth century, it broke out into open warfare.

Genoa was a much older city than Venice. While the latter was undergoing her birth pangs in the northern Adriatic, the character of the Genoese on the other side of the Italian peninsula was being tempered in the fires of adversity.

When the city of Rome was in her heyday, Genoa enjoyed a lively trade bringing luxury goods from Africa. In 205 B.C. she helped defend Rome against the Carthaginians under Hannibal. For her pains she was

razed to the ground by Hannibal's brother Mago. But
Rome, not ungrateful, helped Genoa rebuild, then made
her a capital of a municipium (a province of the empire)
known as the Ligurian Republic.

By 193 A.D. she was an important commercial force in
the Roman Empire's network of trade. Her ships plied
the coastal routes between southern Gaul (landing at
present-day Marseilles) and Rome itself, as well as cruising
south, along the African coast.

The Genoese continued to prosper until the fifth century. Then the barbarians swept down into the Empire
from the north and finally overturned Roman rule. Once
the Empire had been destroyed, Genoa's far-flung trade
routes were also destroyed.

From the fourth to the sixth centuries, Genoa carried
on a limited commerce with other small coastal towns.
They bartered and bought from one another the neces-
sities of life—grain, maize, and fish.

During the sixth and seventh centuries, while Venice
was expanding her trade in the Adriatic, the waters off
the coast of Genoa (known today as the Tyrrhenian Sea)
were plagued by constant attacks by the Saracens. These
infidels from the coast of Africa, lured by the magnificent
harbor, sacked the city periodically, as did the Norman
raiders coming all the way from England. One Norman
chief pretended to have died, had the townspeople invited to his funeral, then rose from his bier in full armor
and slaughtered them. The Saracens put their city to the
torch and their wives and children to the sword. For
many years, as strangers approached, the Genoese ran and
hid in caves in the hills. Then they built boats so that

A Saracen warrior   they could make their escape to the sea.

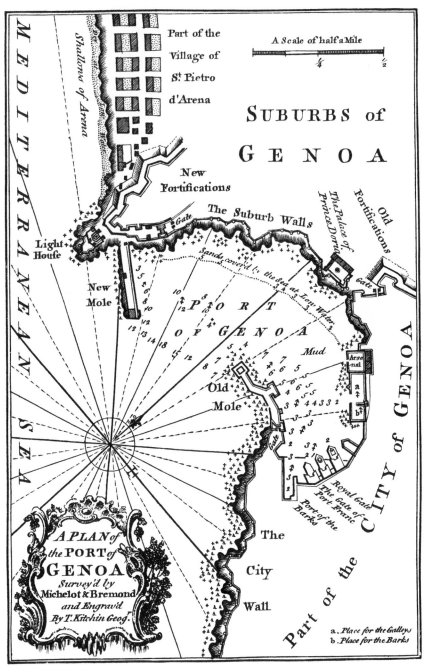

A PLAN of the PORT of GENOA Survey'd by Michelot & Bremond and Engrav'd By T. Kitchin Geog.

Map of Genoa's harbor shows importance of city wall as a protection.

The continuing menace of these pagans finally roused the Genoese from their apathy. The merchants were forced to protect themselves. They set to work to make their city impregnable. They built and fortified a wall that encircled the town and ran right down to the shores of the harbor. The wall proved to have a psychological as well as a military value. The city had not known such a feeling of security and strength since the glorious days of the Roman Empire. This was the first step she took to regain her place as a powerful city-state.

The second step involved her reentry into active trading in the Mediterranean. Powerful bishops were the first to see that the Genoese got money to build more boats so that they could retaliate against the infidels. When the Pope, in the sixth century issued his order to the city-states to rid the neighboring seas of the Saracens, the Genoese, seeing the chance to rid themselves of the shadow of an ancient enemy, were quick to respond.

Also enlisted in the Pope's campaign was Pisa, a city-state that, for many years, was a commercial rival of Genoa's. Both cities from time to time launched attacks

Much of Genoa, like this church, was built on or close to the sea.

on Sardinia and Corsica, islands where the Saracens often
put in for water and food. Pisa rapidly drove them from
Sardinia. Genoa was not so quick to wrest Corsica from
the Moors, but she, too, finally won a foothold in the
neighboring island.

The artistic artisans
of Pisa liked detail.

The possibility of once more becoming a leader in
Mediterranean trade excited the Genoese. They were not
content to stop with Corsica. Sardinia, under the influence of Pisa, held no promise. Was there another direction in which to expand?

The Genoese were aware that the Lombards, from the
northwest corner of Italy, were trading by overland route
with the western Europeans. Genoa had once controlled
this trade. Why not again? Rather than compete with
Pisa and Amalfi, whose merchants were trading building
materials and arms to the Arabs of Africa in return for
slaves, the merchants of Genoa decided to renew their
old connections with the trading centers in southern
France.

Members of the house of Doria, for example, one of
the leading financial families of Genoa, journeyed often
to the provinces of southern France. Each spring and

Pope Urban II gave Corsica to Pisa, a move which Genoa later contested.

fall a Doria ship sailed to Marseilles. They attended the fairs to trade with the merchants of Europe and then returned to Genoa to sell European wares to traders there. But this trade with the Europeans was not the only commerce in which the Genoese were involved. Time passed. Genoa realized that more and more goods were available on the eastern shores of the Mediterranean, and to keep up she must compete with Pisa. While the Genoese businessmen had concentrated on the western trade, the Pisans had developed a flourishing commerce to the east. If Genoa did not soon carve out for herself a share of this traffic, she would have lost for all time any chance of regaining the position of leadership she had enjoyed in the days of the Roman Empire.

The Genoese plan was twofold. Her merchants would open new markets in the eastern Mediterranean, especially in the Levant. At the same time, they would continue to strengthen their hold on Corsica. That island possessed many excellent harbors where ships bound for ports in Africa and the Levant could be supplied. They realized that this colony of theirs was of the greatest commercial importance.

But Pisa, too, recognized the value of Corsica. Sardinia was not enough to satisfy her. So, in 1091, her citizens persuaded Pope Urban II to cede the island to her. The Corsicans, however, remained loyal to the Genoese who had freed them from the tyranny of the Moors. They refused to submit to the papal order. Next, they turned to Genoa for help. With this incident, a rivalry began that would help prepare Genoa for an even greater struggle with Venice.

Each republic intercepted the shipping of its foe. Each sought to drive the other out of Corsica. But neither was powerful enough to deliver the decisive blow. The war dragged on with no one really gaining any significant advantage.

In the midst of this fruitless conflict Urban II died, and a new Pope, Calixtus II, came to power in Rome. Genoa and Pisa were pledged to the defense of Rome. Calixtus began to fear that if they both exhausted all their strength fighting each other, they would leave Rome open to attack from the Saracens. To avoid such a disaster he invited them to a peace council at the Vatican.

To represent her, Genoa sent a recorder of annals named Caffaro; Pisa dispatched her hot-headed Archbishop Roger to plead her case. Roger cited theological reasons for Pisa's claim to Corsica. He maintained that, according

Pope Urban II speaks
to a kneeling peti-
tioner.

to canon law, property granted by one Pope could not
be denied by another. He listed an impressive array of
precedents to support his assertion. From a legal standpoint Roger was right. His presentation, though heated,
was sound. But the outcome in such disputes does not
always depend on justice.

Caffaro knew that there was no legal reason to justify
Genoa's claim to Corsica, so he wasted no time in trying
to present one. Besides, everyone knew how impressive
Roger was when dealing with canon law. Caffaro chose
another approach. He was the product of a people
dedicated to business; he knew that all things have a
price. Therefore he settled on a scheme whereby he
would try to buy the papal decision.

Roger had just made a speech of particular violence.
When he had finished, Caffaro accompanied the Pope and
his cardinals to their chamber. The door to the anteroom

Pope Calixtus II

Caffaro was a man who knew that all kinds of things could be bought.

closed. The Genoan addressed the group:

"Your Worships, this is not a question of canon law. My people freed the Corsicans from the heathens. Naturally, these good Christian people wish to remain subjects of their liberator. Let us here not ask the Corsicans to accept the rule of foreigners who have done nothing for them."

Caffaro paused judiciously, then continued: "As a token of the esteem in which Genoa and Corsica hold your most honored persons, I have been instructed to leave this gift with you. I look forward to what I am certain will be a fair decision." With these words he placed a velvet pouch in the offering box hanging on the wall near the door and abruptly strode from the room.

The College of Cardinals at last met to announce its decision. Genoa was awarded custody of Corsica. When he heard the news, Archbishop Roger raged and fumed. He flung his miter (hat) and sacred ring at the Pope's feet and rushed from the court, crying out, "I'll be no Archbishop of yours!"

The Pisans, upon learning of the bribery, refused to accept the Council's findings. Once again the war was

Pope Innocent III

resumed.   But now Pisa found herself at a great disadvantage.   She was under the papal ban; the papal allies hemmed her in on all sides.   Her ships were wrecked; her crews were beaten; her commerce was curtailed.

When yet another new Pope, Innocent II, summoned both Genoa and Pisa to agree to a peaceful settlement, Pisa accepted willingly enough.   The struggle cost Pisa her advantage over Genoa in many of the Mediterranean markets, with the exception of Corsica which she was to share with Genoa.

The arrangement did not last long.   Toward the middle of the twelfth century Frederick Barbarossa ("Red Beard"), a powerful German ruler whose dominion already extended over central Europe and much of northern Italy, set out to take over Genoa.   In his first attempt to conquer the city he was unsuccessful.   He invited Pisa to come in on his side, an action that proved to be the spark igniting a smoldering flame.

Medieval French representation of Crusaders.

Again Pisa and Genoa fell on one another's shipping; they terrorized each other's crews.   So continued the history of the two part-time combatants.   The incidents

varied, but the pattern remained unchanged: intrigues, broken peace treaties, and a series of inconclusive encounters.

Meanwhile, Genoa's strength as a maritime power was being given a tremendous boost by events in Europe. In the year 675 the infidels had taken Jerusalem, the Holy City, so named because Christ's body was buried there. For a time Christians were allowed to come and go as they pleased, and in the western world not too much attention was given to it. But, over a period of several centuries, the Christians in Jerusalem began to be persecuted. Finally, when they were barred from the city altogether, feelings ran high.

By this time, it should be remembered, Christianity had spread from Rome throughout western Europe. The plight of Christian worshippers caused restless murmurings among the devout that would later flower into the Crusades.

A fanatical character, named Peter of Amiens but better known as "Peter the Hermit," traveled about Europe stirring up leaders to organize a crusade that would sail to the Holy Land and wrest it from the grip of the infidels. A number of wealthy lords, kings, and princes from the lands that are now France, England, Germany, Belgium, and Holland responded. In 1095 Peter got the ear of Pope Urban II. The Pope gave him permission to come to Rome and preach in the open air.

Peter must have been a spellbinder, for his harangue was a fantastic success. He aroused some 100,000 listeners to a frenzy of zeal. They went away crying, "On to Jerusalem!"

A picture of what life was like during the years when

Picture in medieval
manuscript of ships
and town.

these events took place may be helpful in understanding
what follows. In the western hemisphere, it was, with
few exceptions, mainly the area bordering on the Mediterranean that could be called civilized. To the north,
following the collapse of the Roman Empire, chaos had
reigned. With the exception of certain isolated areas,
conditions were primitive. Powerful princes acquired
sway over vast expanses of land, only to give way after
a few years to some other ruler. But the real power rested
in the hands of feudal lords on whom the kings and princes
depended for support. Great wealth in land and goods
was concentrated in their hands. For the serf or peasant,
life was rough and hard, little better than slavery.

The people living around the Mediterranean for the
most part were realistic and practical. The feudal lords
of the north, however, could be moved by emotional
tides. They lived by concepts such as noblesse oblige (the

Crusaders debark,
ready to fight for
Jerusalem.

obligation of the nobility to be kind and helpful to those below them in class and rank), codes of chivalry, and combat for the sake of honor.

The idea of a Crusade fired their imaginations. The lords and princes gathered together huge hosts. They could march down through Europe, but they needed ships to transport the knights and their followers to Jerusalem.

Who was better suited for this role than the Genoese who already had a long history of war against the Saracens? Money was made available to build up Genoa's maritime strength.

In 1096, fragments of the First Crusade began to trickle forth. In the following year, Genoa sent twelve galleys to transport troops of the two leaders of the Crusade, Godfrey of Bouillon and the Count of Flanders, to the Holy Land.

The Genoan contingent was headed by a popular hero, Guglielmo Embriarcko, who, among his other gifts, appears to have been an inventive engineer. The city of Antioch (in what is now Turkey) fell to the Crusaders after a stubborn siege, largely because of the catapults, storming towers, and other machines of war that he designed and built.

Jerusalem fell on July 15, 1099. Godfrey, who refused the title of king, died shortly thereafter and was succeeded by his brother, Baldwin.

Baldwin, out of gratitude to the Genoese, gave them streets of their own and trading privileges not only in Jerusalem, but in the cities of Joppa, Tyre, Caesarea, and Acre along the eastern shore of the Mediterranean. In return, the Genoese promised to lend their strength to beat off recurrent attacks from the infidels.

So, for the first time, Genoa had a foothold in the eastern Mediterranean. Her position there offered possibilities for immense wealth, for the feudal lords had developed an appetite for the world's goods. Their food was tasteless—they wanted spices; their raiment was plain—they wanted silks, satins, brocades, furs, and other finery; their women were unadorned—they wanted jewels.

These greatly desired items of trade had their point of origin mostly in the east. They came from China, from India, from Persia, from Russia, and from Arabia by caravan or ship, or combinations of both, to the trading ports of the eastern Mediterranean. Venice, through years of patient negotiation, had won trading privileges in the principal trading ports for these goods. But her chief interest lay in her trade with Constantinople in Byzantium, for there a number of well-traveled and profitable caravan routes converged.

One of these routes went north, through Novgorod to the Baltic; another went across the Black Sea to the Sea of Azov. Over the former came furs, the much desired adornment called amber, hides, and cloth; from the latter came the pitch, tar, and resins needed in shipbuilding. And from far-off Cathay (China) came the beautiful silks so greatly sought after, along with pepper, cinnamon, and other spices from the Indies.

Meanwhile, feelings between Genoa and Pisa continued to smolder. Pisa, too, had been granted trading privileges in the East, and throughout this period she remained Genoa's chief rival. Things came to a head one morning early in the year 1296. Two large fleets, one Pisan, one Genoese, suddenly encountered each other. The bulk of

A 13th century knight

each city-state's naval force was thus committed.

At that time, a naval battle was fought something like this: The fleets consisted of galleys propelled with oars that were usually manned by slaves—120 or so to a ship —and sailing ships called nefs. The latter were lateen-rigged—equipped with triangular sails. Nefs and galleys alike had strong sharp beaks at the prow with which they hoped to ram their foes in combat. The nefs had two full decks, half-decks, and quarter-decks towering high fore and aft. Five nefs could carry 7,000 men-at-arms.

The two fleets usually approached each other with all ships either spread out in a straight line or deployed in facing crescents. Each ship maneuvered for a position with its bow pointing toward the side of an enemy ship, the best position from which to ram.

While the ships were still some distance from each other, the artillery barrage began. This salvo consisted of large rocks or chunks of metal, weighing about 150 pounds each, hurtled toward the enemy by catapult.

From about the same distance vessels then let go with a weapon called "Greek fire." This seems to have been an ancient version of the modern Molotov cocktail, a collection of rags soaked in oil and other flammables wrapped around a stick, so that they could be thrown like a spear or shot from a crossbow.

Each ship had only a single chance to ram. Once that chance was lost, the next move was to try to board the enemy. At that moment other ingenious means were employed. Decks were flooded with liquid soap so that the boarders would slip and fall. Meanwhile some of the attacking crew, counterparts of modern frogmen, would slide overboard and try to bore, chop, or smash a hole

in the hull of an enemy ship which might cause her to
sink. The next and final phase, where the issue was often
decided, was hand-to-hand combat.

During this particular battle, the Pisans had superior
strength, and it looked as though victory would be theirs.
But concealed behind the nearby island of Meloria, the
Genoese had a large number of ships. The battle was
joined. The Pisans thought they were winning when
suddenly the Genoese reserves appeared. The shock and
surprise tipped the scales. In the end the Genoese utterly
routed the Pisans.

The battle of Meloria was decisive. Genoa no longer
had anything to fear from her rival neighbor. The back-
bone of Pisa's strength had been broken. Not only had
Genoa defeated her rival, but she had emerged from the
battle with a powerful fleet of ships, left more or less
intact, at her disposal. She was now ready to challenge
Venice for control of the eastern trade.

Now the true nature of the Genoese character was to
be revealed—a factor that would drastically affect the
future course of events.

Politically, the structures of Genoa and Venice were
somewhat similar. Both were really oligarchies, ruled in
fact by a handful of wealthy and noble families. To the
average Venetian, however, the city was his life. Venice
fired his imagination, demanded his utmost loyalty, and,
for his industry and bravery, rewarded him handsomely.
The average Genoese was, above all, an individualist. He
considered his rights not as something to expect from a
benevolent, all-powerful city entity, but as something to
fight for. Moreover, the city was split into nobles and
commoners. As a result, Genoa was wracked by internal

strife and factional disputes that greatly handicapped her growth. At sea, however, this same fierce individualistic spirit incited her seamen to dare, to venture far, to challenge the unknown.

As soon as Genoa was free from fear of attack by Pisa, her sailors set out, sailing first along the coast of North Africa. There they established colonies in former Saracen strongholds. Reaching Spain, they established bases. Some even sailed out through the Straits of Gibraltar, a great adventure in those days. Genoese sailors laid claim to the Canary Islands and the Azores. One party of explorers, led by two brothers named Vivaldo, left the Azores searching for a new route to the fabled east several centuries ahead of Christopher Columbus. They were never heard from again.

An Italian nobleman, richly clad

Venice, with the activities by which she lived carried on at sea away from her shores, managed for many years to remain free of the intrigues, feuds, invasions, and counter-invasions that took so much of the energy of other city-states at that time. To the Venetian, life was good, and there were good things to be had if one were bold, industrious, practical, tenacious, and realistic.

Venice was now indeed "the island city that had become the jewel box of the world." Or, in the words of Alexander Pope, an eighteenth-century English poet:

> Mark by what wretched steps their glory grows
> From dirt and seaweed as proud Venice rose.

Many of the luxury goods that Venice handled to her profit were passed along to the ultimate consumer. But many of them also remained at home to make the splendor

The lion rampant was the symbol of S. Marco.

PAX TIBI MARCE EVANGELISTA MEUS

of Venice unique in all the civilized world. From the artful mosaics that decorated the piazzas and the floors of public buildings or the courtyards of palaces and private homes to the silvered towers that graced the skyline, the Venetian was reminded everywhere he looked of his city's greatness. Venice had shops and bazaars unsurpassed in the world. Crafts flourished. The secrets of Venetian glassblowers were closely guarded. She gained renown for her leather goods and her furniture.

The wealth of her citizens staggers the imagination. The profit on a single transaction was anywhere from 20 to 40 percent. At one time there were several hundred merchants whose annual income ranged between 200,000 and 500,000 ducats per year. The dress of the ruling classes reflected their prosperity. The men wore robes of cloth of a color that indicated their professions, lined within by the most expensive furs. The women indulged their fancies in the most elaborate and ornate headdresses of every kind, richly decorated with jewels and gold filigree.

But Venice's continuing prosperity was soon to be disrupted once more—by a force that had nothing to do with trade.

Genoa Comes
to the Fore

The trouble began in 1159. In that year the Pope died, and the cardinals convened to elect his successor. From the very beginning the College of Cardinals was torn by opposing factions. Two candidates, Cardinal Roland and Cardinal Octavian, appeared equally qualified to wear the papal miter, but neither could muster the necessary support. In the end each declared himself Pope: Roland assumed the title Pope Alexander III, and Octavian called himself Pope Victor IV. The situation at Rome became further strained and finally degenerated into an exchange of insults. At length, each Pope excommunicated the other. Thereupon, all Christendom took sides.

It is well to remember that the affairs of the Church were not separated from political concerns or daily business life as they are now. In those days one could not function without the other. The most intimate relationship between the two was characterized by the Holy Roman Empire.

While political chaos reigned throughout Europe, following the collapse of the old Roman Empire, there was no central authority and no unity. So, as the Catholic Church grew, gaining more followers and more power,

A mounted Crusader

Pope Alexander III

many Europeans saw this new religious empire as a framework of order that might replace the structure vacated by the Caesars.

The German royal family, the house of Hohenstaufen, proposed to rule in the worldly sense while the Pope looked after the spiritual concerns of this empire. Although not always so holy and well-ordered as it might have been, the structure of the Holy Roman Empire roughly amounted to this: A Roman Pope and a German Emperor, their destinies fused together for better or for worse.

When the situation of the dual Popes developed in 1159, Barbarossa, the same German monarch who earlier had rekindled the Pisa–Genoa feud, had to make up his mind which pope he would support. Barbarossa made his decision at last. He threw in his lot with Pope Victor IV.

Throughout this uproar, Venice, "the cat who always walked by itself," remained coolly aloof. Germany, Hungary, Bohemia, Norway, and Sweden supported Victor.

Finally, Venice recognized Alexander, Victor's rival, as Pope. The repercussions were immediate. Incensed, Frederick Barbarossa at once moved to seize Grado, one of Venice's important colonies along the coast. He forced an ally of his, the Patriarch of Aquileja, to attack it. But the proud Venetians were not to be so easily put down. The city-state dispatched her galleys to the aid of the beleaguered city. Her forces seized the Patriarch with twelve of his cannon and 700 of his soldiers. Grado was hers once more.

Venice did not allow the struggle with her old foe "Red

Frederick Barbarossa, head of the Holy Roman Empire.

Beard" to rest here. She persuaded her neighbors Verona, Vicenza, and Padua to refuse to pay the tribute due Barbarossa as the Emperor of the Holy Roman Empire. This so-called Veronese League joined the League of Lombard Cities in 1167 in an alliance against the Germans. According to its terms, if any one of the members were attacked or threatened by the Emperor, they would all declare war on him.

Barbarossa was furious. The rulers of the Empire had always done their best to keep Italy's city-states warring among themselves. Divided, they were weak and therefore easy to control. United, they could be a formidable foe. In Barbarossa's eyes, Venice was the architect of this alliance. He swore that he would crush her. But it wasn't all that easy. He was reluctant to start a fight with governments who were supposedly within his sphere of influence. At last he brought the problem to the attention

Venetian ships engage in one of their great sea battles.

of his minister of finance.   The latter was quick to point
out the obvious solution: He could destroy Venice all
right, if he could undermine the source of her strength—
trade.

Barbarossa thereupon undertook to bring about the
financial ruin of Venice.   In 1170, as autumn approached,
two special emissaries left Barbarossa's palace carrying
secret papers to Manuel II, ruler of the Byzantine Empire, in Constantinople.   Although no one knows exactly
what these papers contained, legend has it that they in-
spired the ruthless behavior that followed.

Emperor Manuel was jealous of Venice's success.   He
liked to recall the days when the city had been only too
happy to put her ships at the disposal of the powerful

One of the Crusaders
who sailed from
Venice.

eastern Emperor, as little more than a vassal. To be sure, that had been a long time ago, but Manuel felt that it could be so again.

Peace is reached between Alexander III and Frederick Barbarossa.

He brooded over the fact that Venice had risen to power largely because of the prosperity she enjoyed in her trade with Constantinople. He relished the stories he had heard as a youth concerning Venice's humiliation at the hands of the pirates. It irked him further to consider that Venice had long since recovered from these blows.

Manuel had seethed in silence long enough. In the predawn hours of March 12, 1171, the Emperor summoned his chief of police. Together they went over the plan they had been developing for several months. Timing was essential.

Long ago the Byzantine Emperor had granted to Venice

a separate section or quarter in the city of Constantinople. Here Venetian mercantile families had lived for
generations. Except for the absence of canals, one might
have thought one was in Venice. The architecture was
the same, the manner of dress and living in general was
the same. The Venetians had their own laws and their
own government to which they paid their taxes. The
overseas Venetians differed little from those at home.
They felt themselves immune from any interference, large
or small, on the part of local authorities.

It came as a complete surprise to the local inhabitants
when shortly after sunrise the police and militia invaded
the quarter and began a house-to-house search. By nightfall the Venetians who had not fled were jammed into the
city jails. The overflow was housed in neighboring
monasteries. This same scene was reenacted at almost
the same moment in every Venetian colony throughout
Byzantium. In a few hours Venice had lost the fruits
of fifty years of work.

The Genoese were overjoyed. The Byzantium trade
was all theirs. Wooing Emperor Manuel had paid off
at last. The power Venice had once enjoyed in the
empire now passed to her—so she thought. Manuel went
so far as to invite the Genoese to occupy the warehouses
and piers from which the Venetians had been ousted.
Genoa could now take title to the extremely profitable
Black Sea trade. Moreover, Barbarossa had successfully
reduced Venice's power.

Barbarossa was, nevertheless, later forced to recognize
Alexander III's claim to the Papacy. Alexander III had
not only shown himself a better man than his rival Victor,
but had outlived him. On July 24, 1176, the schism

formally came to an end. In a mass performed in San
Marco, that great historic basilica in Venice, Alexander
lifted the excommunication from Frederick while the
latter pledged Pope Alexander his support.

This was cold comfort to Venice. Although she had
won the contest over the competing Popes, she had lost
her richest trading arrangement.

The Holy War
of the French

Pope Innocent III was troubled. The Third Crusade had failed. The infidels still held Jerusalem; Christians there were still being persecuted. He would make one more effort to wrest the Holy City from heathen hands. In the year 1200 he issued a decree (known as a Papal Bull) announcing the Fourth Crusade.

The influential barons of France—the Count of Champagne, the Count of Flanders, and the Count of Blois—responded to the Pope's call. They in turn enlisted the support of the powerful knights and lords who were their neighbors.

Now the sponsors of the crusade faced the problem of transporting their troops to the Holy Land. It would be too time-consuming, expensive, and dangerous to transport them via the land route eastward across Europe and then south through Asia Minor. The best solution seemed to be to send them by sea across the Mediterranean. With this end in view it was decided to approach the city of Venice. The three counts of France therefore dispatched six envoys to carry on negotiations in their behalf.

It was cold that day in February, 1201, when the richly-clad foreigners arrived in the city. Unaccustomed to the dampness of the winter winds blowing in from the Adriatic, the noblemen from France gathered their silken robes close to their bodies and walked quickly along the sidewalks by the canals. They had changed from their heavy woolen traveling clothes at the inn where they had stabled their horses.

The ambassadors wanted to impress the Venetians with their splendor and elegance when they stepped from the slender boat that brought them to the Rialto. If they were going to ask to be outfitted for the Fourth Crusade, they wished to look as if they were to be trusted with such a worthy cause. They had been looking forward to meeting the Doge, but the chill seemed to dampen their spirits. To onlookers the six seemed to be huddled together apologetically, not striding confidently to present their holy mission.

Although the counts did not know it, from the standpoint of the Venetians, they couldn't have come at a more welcome time. Trade had languished. The city on the Adriatic had not fully recovered from the loss of her

Wealthy Venetians, men and women, wore raiment of great splendor.

Byzantium commerce. She desperately needed a new source of income.

The envoys were received with something less than the enthusiasm that they had expected. The Doge kept them waiting for four days before he would grant them an audience. We have the diary of Geoffrey Villehardouin, one of the French ambassadors, to recount that first, nervous meeting. He described himself as saying,

> Messieurs, we come in the name of the noblest barons of France, who have taken the Cross to avenge the insults to our Lord Jesus Christ, and, if God will, to conquer Jerusalem. No other power on earth can aid us as you can; therefore they implore you, in God's name, to have compassion on the Holy Land, and to join them in avenging the contempt of Jesus Christ by furnishing them with ships and other necessities, so that they may pass the seas.

The Doge Dandolo as a young man

The aging Doge, Enrico Dandolo, had no intention of giving an immediate assent to their request. Although now eighty-five years old and almost blind, he was shrewd and crafty. The outfitting of such a sizable force offered an unparalleled opportunity for Venice to fill her empty coffers. Ships and arms! She could supply them, all right. The envoys had come to the right place.

As was his custom when deep in thought, he slowly twisted round and round the famous ruby ring that he wore on the index finger of his left hand. Then, allowing both hands to rest in the folds of his scarlet silken cloak, he inquired softly, "What are the terms on which you wish to secure our aid?" There was a silence. He raised his eyebrows. "Surely," he said, "you do not intend that we bear this great expense alone."

Dandolo, accustomed by his long experience as a merchant to negotiating financial matters, planned to drive a hard bargain in the end. But first he would enjoy playing upon the French love of ceremony and ritual.

"The matter is too momentous for one old man to decide by himself," he said with a sigh. "We must discuss it with our ministers. I will call a special meeting of the Grand Council. Come back a week from now and I shall have your answer."

The Doge stood up. The audience was over. The Frenchmen were escorted from the Ducal Palace. They were quite pleased with themselves. They had presented their case well. The Doge appeared agreeable to their plan.

While the French envoys waited anxiously, Venice blazed with excitement over the prospects of a new Crusade. At every wineshop, at every dinner table, it was the one topic of conversation. Twice the Grand Council, the ruling congressional body of Venice, met behind closed doors. Then, six days later, the Doge convened a meeting of one thousand leading Venetian citizens in the vast piazza before the beautiful San Marco Cathedral to pray for guidance. Enrico Dandolo was indeed setting the stage with great dramatic instinct for this, the most important decision of his career.

Dandolo heightened the Frenchmen's anxiety by making them wait one day more. Finally, on the eighth day, the Doge summoned the envoys. He informed them that the Grand Council had voted to support their appeal. However, they themselves would be required to present the request to the Venetian populace.

"Bear in mind," Dandolo said, "that Venice is a republic. In any matter as important as this one, the citizens themselves must decide."

Then, almost casually, Enrico Dandolo mentioned what was to him the most critical point in the agreement—the price.

Transportation of 4,500 knights and their horses, 9,000 squires, and 20,000 men-at-arms would be provided for one year at the rate of four marks for each horse and two marks for each man—a total of 85,000 silver marks. (It is difficult to make an exact comparison, but the price would be in the neighborhood of millions of dollars today.) Everything was specified to the decimal point; so much grain per day per horse; so much bread and wine per day per foot soldier. The Doge also stipulated that, of all the lands, goods, and materials of war taken from the infidels, one-half would go to Venice.

The envoys, none of them experienced businessmen, agreed. As this second meeting came to a close, Doge Dandolo himself was able to be exact about the moment when all would be ready.

"As to the date of departure, we will have fifty-two fully manned galleys ready to sail on June 29. When you return with your knights and foot soldiers, we expect you to have the money with you."

The Doge, hesitating only long enough to catch his breath, continued. "Tomorrow at noon I will summon all Venetians to the Church of San Marco. At that meeting you will declare yourselves to the people. Until tomorrow, gentlemen, good day and good fortune."

The next day, the lamps hanging on their chains from the great vaulted ceiling of San Marco's cast pallid pools of light on a sea of faces as the Venetians gathered in the

unheated church.   The citizens of Venice were not unaccustomed to seeing the strange dress and finery of foreign
lands.   They examined the robed and plumed French
nobles with the critical eyes of those accustomed to the
comings and goings of pilgrims and princes, merchants
and beggars, from all over the civilized world.

Geoffrey Villehardouin, spokesman for the French,
moved to the front of the main altar and prepared to
speak.   He marveled at the 7,000 jewels of the famous
altar which reflected flickering candle light in multicolored
stone.   Then he turned to face the hushed crowd, drew
a deep breath, and began:

Geoffrey Villehar-
douin, a leader of the
Crusade, recorded the
events.

> Messieurs, the noblest and most powerful of France have
> sent us to pray you to take pity on Jerusalem in bondage
> to the Turk, and to crave that for God's love ye aid us
> to avenge the shame of Jesus Christ; for they know that
> no other nation is so mighty on the sea as yours; and
> therefore have they charged us to kneel before you till
> ye have granted their prayer and had pity on the Holy
> Land.

With that, all six envoys fell down upon their knees before
the Venetians and wept.

Enrico Dandolo saw that his people were moved by
Villehardouin's eloquence. His reference to Venice as the
most powerful force on the sea had flattered them. As
an able politician the Doge took the cue. He rose, moved
toward the still kneeling French, and began the chant:

"*Concediamo!* (We grant it.) *Concediamo!*" Immediately the people caught the word and thundered it
throughout the sanctuary, "*Concediamo! Concediamo!*"

Dandolo allowed the enthusiasm to swell. Then, as the
cry reached a frenzied crescendo, he extended his right
arm and with his hand outstretched he hushed the
throng. He turned to the French and motioned for them
to stand. Shifting the folds of his long ducal robe, he
turned to face the congregation again and intoned,

> The greatest nation upon earth has left all other peoples
> and elected your company, that together we should share
> in this great enterprise, even in the deliverance of our
> Lord.

The Venetians had every reason to be pleased. The
agreement with the Crusaders would bring them a wind-

fall beyond their expectations—and at a time when it was badly needed.

In the first decade of the twelfth century, the Doge Falier had decreed the creation in Venice of a state-owned arsenal, a vast industrial complex to be devoted to the building of ships and the manufacture of arms. For the former purpose Venetians could draw upon the forests inland and across the Adriatic on the Dalmatian coast. For the latter, she had the steel of Damascus, the finest in the world.

Now the arsenal sprang to life. Hammers rang, and forges glowed. New ships were built and slid down the ways. Old ones were caulked and made seaworthy again. Oars were fashioned and sails repaired. Meanwhile, swords, halberds, and pikes such as the knights and feudal lords of Europe had never known were being fashioned for their use against the infidels. The Venetians were moving steadily toward fulfillment of their end of the bargain.

But an impasse developed when the envoys were called upon to pay. They did not have with them the sum that the Venetians were asking. They were short of the estimated cost by 34,000 marks.

The Crusaders Lay Siege to Constantinople

Months passed while the Venetians busied themselves building the needed ships and waited for the arrival of the main army of the Fourth Crusade. An enormous camp was set up on the mainland where the newcomers would be accommodated—for a fee.

From all over Europe they straggled in and settled down to wait. But they did not appear in the numbers anticipated. In many places, in many ways, things had gone wrong. Theobald, Count of Champagne, who was to have led the Crusade, died suddenly and his successor failed to match him in zeal. A large contingent of Crusaders leaving Bruges, Belgium, broke the agreement and headed for Marseilles and Genoa to be outfitted instead of showing up at Venice. Other groups either made separate arrangements or did not come at all. The Crusaders who were on hand grew restless and unruly at the enforced idleness.

But at last a considerable force was at hand, and the Venetians had everything in readiness. Because of their diminished numbers, however, the Crusaders found it impossible to raise the necessary funds. When this situation was made known to the Doge, he refused to set sail

until the money was paid.   Everything remained at a
stalemate.   The cunning old statesman, however, was
reluctant to forego entirely this unique opportunity for
profit; it was one that might not soon come again.   He
sent for the French envoys.   Then he proposed a compromise plan that he felt quite certain would satisfy the
needs of both parties.

Some years before, following the crushing of the pirates,
the Venetians had brought under their sphere of influence
much of the Dalmatian coast across the Adriatic.   But
in 1166 the key port Zara on the Dalmation coast had
revolted against the Venetian yoke.   If Venice were to
regain control of Zara and retain control of other ports
along the coast, she would have to reconquer Zara and
teach her a lesson.   Much more than Zara was at stake.

Dandolo presented a way out for the Crusaders.   Why
shouldn't they make up the deficit by serving the cause
of Venice as fighting men?   If the barons would stop on
the way to the Holy Land long enough to help the Doge
conquer Zara, he would see to it that the fleet sailed
immediately.

The Crusaders balked.   They were being asked to
attack Christians, not heathens.   They had not left their
homes and their loved ones and traveled so far to keep
the peace in Venice's colonial household.   They were after
infidels.   The Doge's proposal, as they saw it, asked for
an outrageous detour from their spiritual goal—the liber-
ation of Jerusalem.   But what recourse had they?   They
had no hope of getting up the needed marks.   The knights
of the Crusade had plenty of land and castles but no ready
cash.   Before they left home, they had already sold
practically everything they owned to finance their own

retinues. They had no choice but to accept the Doge's terms or abandon the Crusade.

It was a beautiful, crisp day, October 3, 1202, when the knights of the Fourth Crusade were ready to venture forth. The Venetian men-of-war were moored by the quays, their gangplanks down to receive the warriors. The golden lion of St. Mark on his crimson field snapped in the breeze from every towering flagstaff.

The knights marched for the last time through the streets to the notes of a hundred silver trumpets. The sun gleamed on their breastplates and helmets. It sparkled on the silver trappings of their horses as they were loaded below decks—a most unusual sight to Venetian eyes.

The Doge had mustered a fleet of 480 vessels. Some, about 140 feet long, were the largest afloat at that time. They were so heavy that, in addition to their sails, it took fifty oars in three decks, four men to an oar, to propel them. Their sides, bedecked with the shields and multicolored emblems of the crusading knights, were a pageant of heraldry. The knights stood leaning over the railings of the deck, waving and shouting to the citizens massed along the canals. Aloft, the masts were bright with pennants and flags, the colors of the noble lords. And

Rowel spurs such as these were worn by the Crusaders.

atop the tallest mast of every ship flew the banner of the Sacred Cross.

Slowly the procession of ships made its way down the harbor toward the lagoon. The Venetians on shore, dressed in their finest silks and satins, waved and cheered the Crusaders with cries of "On to Jerusalem!" and "Kill the infidels!"

All day the ships moved out, bound for the open sea, until the last one became only a speck on the horizon. Their departure from the City of the Lagoons must have been one of the most dazzling spectacles in all history.

On board one of the ships was Dandolo himself. At the last minute he, too, had decided to accompany the expedition.

A little more than a month later on St. Martin's Eve, November 10, the Crusaders hove to off the harbor of Zara. The attacking force sailed past the breakwater. Knights and men-at-arms swarmed ashore. With such a force, it took little time to subdue the rebellious city. Zara yielded a rich booty. The Crusaders were pleased with their exploit and their share. But Zara was not Jerusalem. The knights were anxious to be moving once more.

Meanwhile, word had reached Pope Innocent in Rome of the attack on Zara. He was so enraged that he excommunicated all the Crusaders. But the expedition repre-

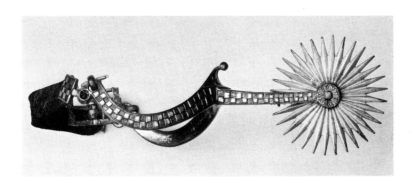

Doge Enrico Dandolo was in his eighties when he outfitted the Crusade.

Enrico Dandolo personally led the Crusaders' assault on Constantinople.

sented the flower of Christendom. It could hardly proceed to carry out the Pope's wishes while under his ban. Finally, after long negotiation, agreement was reached. The Fourth Crusade would be allowed to continue provided there were no more excursions such as Zara.

When word was passed to Dandolo that the Crusaders were now ready to set sail, he stubbornly refused. Dandolo had more than one trick up his sleeve. He called a conference aboard his flagship, the *Paradiso*, at which

he gave his reason: At this time of year the weather in the Adriatic was too unreliable.

"Why are you impatient?" asked the Doge, looking straight at them with his bright but unseeing eyes. "Zara is an excellent wintering place. Food is plentiful and the ships are well protected in this harbor." With his many-ringed right hand he indicated the open waters of the Adriatic.

The French counts grumbled. But again Dandolo had his way. One of the knights growled to his comrade, "Damn that man. Those eyes; it's those eyes. Every time I see him I have the feeling that he is plotting something."

"Yes," agreed his companion, "we are puppets in his hands. We're slaves, aren't we? Our destinies are in the hands of these vile, money-hungry Venetian merchants."

The knight's surmise about the Doge had been correct. He was scheming behind the quiet facade of that inscrutable gaze and the coldly logical words. News had just reached him that a plot was brewing—a plot to overthrow the Emperor of Byzantium. An event like that, properly exploited, could mean the salvation of Venice. For more than thirty years now the merchants of Genoa had dominated the trade in Constantinople while the Venetians continued to smart under the shame of having been shut out of the Empire. Here might be Venice's chance to turn the tables once more.

The moment seemed propitious. It would be most helpful to Dandolo to have the assistance of the Crusaders. But he must find a way to enlist their support without their knowing what he was up to. He must keep the Crusade stalled here at Zara at least for a while.

Next, he would arrange for Alexius, the new claimant to the Byzantine throne, to come in person and present his case to the Crusaders. He had been conspiring with Philip of Swabia (a German kingdom) to arrange for the young man's visit. Dandolo felt certain that Alexius' story would appeal to them. As a boy he had lived in exile. His father, Isaac Comnenus, had once been the Byzantine Emperor. He had been dispossessed of his throne by a power-hungry brother, thrown into prison, and blinded. Now his son was asking only that justice be done, that the rightful claimant be returned to the throne. Who, let alone men committed to righting wrongs, could turn a deaf ear to his plea?

Alexius appeared at Zara just in time. The knights had submitted their final demand that Dandolo put to sea at once. The young Alexius was welcomed aboard the flagship, invited into the war council, and given permission to address the assemblage.

The knights listened in sympathetic silence as Alexius unfolded his distressing tale. He concluded with a ringing, "I will maintain five hundred knights for the perpetual defense of Jerusalem and pay 200,000 silver marks as reparation for your effort."

This generous offer impressed them. The knights held a brief discussion. Then they sent for Dandolo. They suggested, as though they had thought of it themselves, that they stop long enough to subdue Constantinople on the way to the Holy Land. Blandly, the Doge nodded his acquiescence. His scheme to regain control of the vital world trade center was all but complete. And to outward appearances, he had not so much as lifted a finger.

This plan was in direct contradiction of Pope Innocent's orders. How had Dandolo managed it? By pleading the righteousness of Alexius' cause? Or by painting alluring pictures of the rich booty to be had in Constantinople? At any rate, after a short pause, the fleet set out from the island of Corfu in April, 1203, to assault the city on the Bosporus.

"There were all the transports and galleys of the host," wrote Villehardouin, "and many a merchant ship. The day was fair and clear; the wind gentle and mild. And verily it seemed that the fleet must subdue the land, for so far as the eye could reach naught could be seen save the sails of ships and of vessels, so that men's hearts did much rejoice."

It appeared, however, that the fleet would not so easily subdue Constantinople. The high, thick stone walls with a double moat up to now had enabled the city to beat off all invaders. Never, since those walls were built, had the city been taken.

The French were not accustomed to sea travel nor to large ports. As they first laid eyes on the great capital of Byzantium, they were filled with both fear and admiration. "When they saw the length and breadth of the town, which was the Queen of Cities," says our chronicler Villehardouin, "there was none so bold but his flesh crept."

The attack in the harbor, begun early on a fine July morning, got off to a good start. The invaders were able to slip the chain that guarded its mouth. Five days later, however, when the French pressed a land attack on the city itself, all did not go so smoothly. But the Doge was

Ancient parchment shows Crusaders approaching and attacking Constantinople.

not one to stand by and see triumph elude his grasp. Edward Gibbon, the eighteenth-century historian, has described the sea attack launched by the doughty Doge.

On the side of the harbour the attack was more successfully conducted by the Venetians; and that industrious people employed every resource that was known and

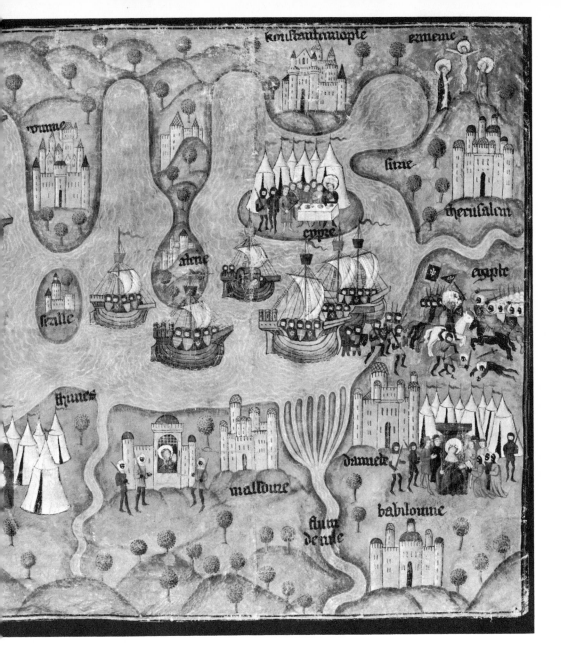

practiced before the invention of gunpowder. A double
line, three bowshots in front, was formed by the galleys
and ships; and the swift motion of the former was supported by the weight and loftiness of the latter, whose
decks and poops and turrets were the platforms of military
engines that discharged their shot over the heads of the
first line. The soldiers who leaped from the galleys on

shore immediately planted and ascended their scaling-
ladders, while the large ships, advancing more slowly into
the intervals and towering a drawbridge, opened a way
through the air from their masts to the rampart. In the
midst of the conflict the Doge's venerable and conspicuous
form stood aloft in complete armour on the prow of the
galley. . . . His vessel was the first that struck, and
Dandolo was the first warrior on shore. . . . On a sudden,
by an invisible hand (for the standard-bearer was probably
slain), the banner of the Republic was fixed on the rampart, twenty-five towers were rapidly occupied, and, by
the cruel expedient of fire, the Greeks were driven from
the adjacent quarter.

The success of the invasion was complete. The dungeon
doors were swung open for the former Emperor, the blind
Isaac. There, in prison, he was reunited with his wife
and his son Alexius.

A few days later Alexius was crowned Emperor. Trouble quickly arose, however. Despite his eloquence,
Alexius was too young and too inexperienced to realize
that he must make adequate provisions for the wishes of
the residents of Constantinople. The old Greek aristoc-
racy refused to accept this upstart who was so friendly
with the Latins.

So, in February, the Greek patriots, led by a noble
nicknamed Martzuphles (shaggy eyebrows) engineered a
successful counterrevolution. The aid Alexius had promised to the Crusade now appeared to be lost. But the
Doge Dandolo, having come this far, was determined not
to give up. Once more he persuaded the Crusaders to
attack Constantinople. He went so far as to offer large
rewards to the first five men who would scale the walls.

The Second Siege of Constantinople began on April 12,

1203.   Dandolo ordered two of the three tallest galleys, the *Pellegrino* and the *Paradiso*, to be lashed together and maneuvered up against one of the city towers.   Platforms had been built between the masts, and these would serve as a gangway for the Venetians to rush onto the top of the tower's wall.   The defenders were so terrified by the sight of this strange-looking machine that they turned in droves and fled.

The population of the defending city numbered almost half a million, the attackers only 20,000.   But by nightfall Constantinople was in the hands of the Crusaders.

What followed is one of the shameful chapters of human history.

The wealth of Constantinople at that time exceeded the riches of all Europe.   Such a prize was too much for the greed of the Crusaders.   They plundered the city without stint.   They tore priceless tapestries from the walls, ripped cloths from the sacred altars, gouged precious jewels from chalices which they used for drinking cups.   They drove horses and mules right into churches to more easily cart away the loot.   Both the Doge and the barons did their best to restrain their followers.   But their threats were unheeded.

The Crusaders did pay from their share of the plunder the rest of the money they still owed the Venetians for transporting them.   They were happy to be free from their obligation to a people for whom they had so little liking.   More important to Venice than the money were

The Rialto, the largest island of Venice, was the center of Venetian trade.

her territorial gains.   It was now possible for her to establish colonies, trading posts, and stations all the way to the
Black Sea.

Not content with her winnings, Venice bought from the
Greeks the isle of Crete, large, fertile, and right in the
center of the Mediterranean between the heel of the
Italian boot and the port of Alexandria in Egypt.   Crete,
thus ideally located, was to become a supply station for
the Venetians on the trade route from any of the ports
of Italy to the Levant, Egypt, and Africa.   Here Venetian
merchants now plied a thriving traffic in silk, spices,
ivory, incense, and other luxury goods.

In one move, largely through the wisdom of her crafty
octogenarian Doge, Venice could lay claim once more to
being the dominant commercial power in the Mediterranean.   She withdrew from the Crusade—which she
foresaw was destined to fail in any event—and concentrated on expanding her commerce.

Her claws, so long sheathed, were now reaching out
toward Genoa.   But Genoa, too, had her hackles up; she
was determined to have it out with Venice and, if possible,
to destroy her once and for all.   For one to exist, ran their
twisted reasoning, the other must be crushed.

The Fourth Crusade never reached Jerusalem.   The
knights found they had all they could manage to keep
the restive city of Constantinople under control.   As for
Venice, although she gained immediate advantage by the
rape of the city, she had irreversibly weakened that out-
post of Christendom.

The Queen of the Adriatic Is Eclipsed

All eyes in the Mediterranean now focused on Crete. Here the two powerful commercial rivals began a struggle that would last for ten generations.

The Venetian government had scarcely moved in on the island when her right to do so was challenged. Some fifty miles to the south of Sicily lies the tiny island of Malta. The Count of Malta was a paunchy, short man with a moustache so bushy it seemed intended to hide his upper lip; he did not cut an impressive figure.

The Count of Malta, Arrigo Pescatore by name, held a very doubtful lordship over Crete. Pescatore had not up to now made much of a point of his authority. He knew he was too weak to enforce his will on a people who lived more than five hundred miles away. But when Venice sent her delegates to take possession of the island, that was the overt move he had been waiting for. He said to himself, "Perhaps fate will deliver me unto my rightful position."

Hitherto it had never greatly concerned Arrigo Pescatore that he was of Genoese origin. Now, suddenly, it mattered very much. With Genoese support he might finally subdue the Cretans. Fully mindful of the smolder-

Venetian merchant-soldier

The famous Piazza of San Marco, as rendered by Francesco Guardi.

ing commercial rivalry between the two city-states, the Count hurried to Genoa to protest the Venetian takeover.

The Ligurian Republic took up the gauntlet on behalf of this petty Count of Malta, not so much because she wished to see justice done, but because she herself had an eye on the island. Genoa, too, wished to use it as a depot and trading post. More especially, she saw the chance to thwart Venice—her hated enemy.

One morning the Genoese fleet appeared off the coast of Crete. Venice maintained a small garrison there under the command of General Rainieri Dandolo. This Dandolo could claim little of the ability exhibited by his relative, the now dead Doge. The General tried half-heartedly to resist, but in the end Crete fell to the invading Genoese.

Rainieri Dandolo himself was captured and hanged.

Genoa was free at last to establish herself on the island and pick up where the Venetians had left off.   But the naval force that had effected the capture of Crete could not remain there long; it was urgently needed elsewhere. Genoa at that moment was busy patrolling her various trading colonies and ports.

In any event, when news reached Venice that Genoa had seized Crete, that republic dispatched her own fleet— one of considerable size—to retake the island.   But this time there was no battle.   The Genoese military were absent, and the inhabitants of undefended Crete had no choice but to submit.   Venice took over without a drop of blood being shed.

Venice now held Crete.   But she was never really able to exploit her advantage.   The Genoese continued to seize her ships and disrupt her trade with Africa and Egypt. In 1218 a rather hollow peace was signed whereby Genoa admitted formally that Crete belonged to Venice.   But even after that the two adversaries continued to seek out and sink each other's ships.   Each incident further fanned the embers of dissension until they burst into flames.

For some time during the thirteenth century Genoa had been pretty well occupied by her battles with Pisa. With her rival disposed of at Meloria in 1296, Genoa's hands were freed.   She could devote all her attention to dealing with her other rival, Venice.

At this point Venice again was waxing fat on her trade in Byzantium.   The prestige, the pomp, the splendor, the immense wealth were slowly being transferred from the jewel of the Bosporus to the bourgeoning City of the Lagoons in the Adriatic.

Street dress of a Ve-
netian nobleman

"Around the square [San Marco Piazza] swarmed an endless current of beggars and nobles, priests and prostitutes, pilgrims and rogues," writes Milton Rugoff in *The Travels of Marco Polo*, giving a vivid picture of Venice in her heyday. For Venice was, like so many medieval cities, a study in violent contrasts: sumptuousness and filth, elegance and coarseness, asceticism and corruption, women who wore gorgeous silks but who went unwashed, gilded palaces without sanitary facilities.

Most fascinating of all were the quays, especially those crowded with goods from far-off places; with cinnamon, cloves, nutmeg, pepper and ginger; with camphor in bamboo tubes; with muslin from Mosul [a province of what is now Turkey], damask from Damascus; with myrrh, rhubarb and sandalwood; with ivory, coral and marble.

Although the piazzas were paved with priceless mosaics, nevertheless, the women of fashion wore high clogs to keep their feet above the muck.

In the fourteenth century, Francesco Petrarch, Italian poet and scholar, wrote, according to Morris Bishop, that he saw vessels

. . . as big as my mansion, their masts taller than its towers. They are mountains floating on the waters. . . . They bear wine to England, honey to Russia, saffron, oil and linen to Assyria, Armenia, Persia and Arabia, wood to Egypt and Greece. They return heavily laden with products of all kinds that are sent from every part of the world.

And, of course with slaves—Circassians [people from a Russian district on the Black Sea], Turks, Russians, Tartars [people from Mongolia]—brought from the Levant

and on the way to the auction market. It was these slaves more than goods or foreigners or details of architecture that tinged Venice with the Orient. An attractive slave girl was worth thousands of dollars because she could also serve as a concubine, and thus the blood of many a Levantine or Caspian type was mingled with that of many a fine Venetian family.

The Doge and his Grand Council receive the poet-statesman, Petrarch.

A vivid description of Venetian trade is given in the old records of the India office in London.

By way of the Syrian ports and of Alexandria came the cloves, nutmegs, mace and ebony of the Moluccas; the sandalwood of Timor; the costly camphor of Borneo; the benzoin of Sumatra and Java; the aloes wood of Cochin China; the perfumes, gums, spices, silks and innumerable curiosities of China, Japan and Siam; the rubies of Pegu;

the fine fabrics of Coromandel; the richer stuffs of Bengal; the spikenard of Nepal and Butan; the diamonds of Golconda; the Damascus steel of Nirmal; the pearls, sapphires, topazes and cinnamon of Ceylon; the pepper, ginger and satinwood of Malabar; the lac, agates, and sumptuous brocades and jewelry of Cambay; the costas and graven vessels, wrought arms and broidered shawls of Cashmere; the bdellium of Scinde; the musk of Thibet; the galbanum of Khorosan; the asafoetida of Afghanistan; the sage penum of Persia; the ambergris, civet and ivory from Zanzibar; the myrrh, balsam and frankincense of Zeila, Berbera and Sheki.

Caravans of trade goods also traveled overland from Venice to the north. And Venetians pioneered in the tourist trade. By making an exclusive contract with the Mohammedans whereby they guaranteed safe conduct, they assured a steady flow of Moslem sightseers to Christian shrines, turning a tidy penny in the process.

At the peak of her power, the merchants of Venice sailed forth in convoys consisting of as many as several hundred ships. They ranged the Adriatic and the Mediterranean, touching at ports along the Levant.

Twice a year two huge convoys known as the Flanders galleys, propelled by sails and oars, sailed through the Straits of Gibraltar bound for Bruges, Belgium. They carried spices, sugar, silks, and other fabrics. On their return voyage their holds were stuffed with wood and fur from Scandinavia, wool from England, and textiles (particularly, linens of all kinds) from the Low Countries.

Every trading expedition that went out was under orders to bring back some object of rarity to add to the glory and enhance the beauty of Venice. The famous bronze horses atop the portico of San Marco that were to become such an attraction to tourists in later centuries were removed bodily from Byzantium during the pillaging. Another treasure was the great altar of San Marco, set with 7,000 jewels. Mosaics, columns of marble, and beautiful stone statues were added bit by bit until the Ducal Palace, the great basilica, public buildings, and private homes became renowned repositories of great art.

Venice prospered from her trading privileges. The royal succession would remain friendly to Venice. For had not a Dandolo lent all his powers to establishing the first of the line on the throne of Byzantium? Genoa, so to speak, was again on the outside.

Unless, of course, the Genoese said to one another, the succession were changed.

It would be a mistake to surmise, however, that because Genoa did nothing, now she was just biding her time. She was too proud and too single-minded in her determination to leave the outcome to chance. She foresaw, sooner than Venice, that a showdown could not much longer be postponed.

Sometime about the mid-1250s Genoa evidently made up her mind to undertake an all-out campaign designed to unseat Venice from her position of privilege in the Byzantine Empire. Her plan needed only the right man to execute it—one who could assure success. The small but powerful group of Genoese merchants dedicated to the enterprise spent a year looking for such a man. At last they found him.

His name was Michael Paleologus. Scion of a noble and distinguished Greek family, his grandparents had been

Michael Paleologus, Greek patriot and ally of Genoa

driven from Constantinople when Dandolo crushed the
Greek uprising in 1203.   As a youth he had been filled
with anger and indignation at the tales he had heard of
how his once-powerful forebears had been driven from
their homeland.   He spent his childhood wandering from
one place to another until, finally, he held a position of
some substance as tutor to John Vatatzes who became the
Emperor of Nicaea, located across the Sea of Marmara
from Constantinople.

It was there that the Genoese secret commission found
Paleologus.   Tall, muscular, handsome, and burning with
political ire, he seemed just the one to lead a revolt.
When the plan was unfolded to him, he accepted with
enthusiasm.   And why not?   Here was a chance to emerge
from obscurity, to avenge the wrongs committed against
his family and friends, and at the same time to embark
on a promising career in his own right, with plenty of
money and power behind him.

The Genoese set up the screen of absolute secrecy
essential to their plan.   Behind it they assembled a powerful military force and sequestered them on ships near the
Byzantine shores.   Then, while the city slept, striking
with the speed and impact of a tornado, this force with
Michael Paleologus at its head swooped down on Constantinople.   The army marched through the empty
streets.   Then it invaded the palace and took over the
government.

Only minutes earlier Emperor Baldwin II had been
awakened.   He fled for his life just before the footsteps
of Paleologus' men echoed through the halls leading to
the royal bedchamber.   The impoverished Baldwin had
put all his trust in the Venetians.   He had counted on

them not only to manage his business affairs and his Empire, but also to see to its defense. The merchants, however, had been far more interested in squeezing what profit they could from the once great and wealthy capital of the East. Now, when Baldwin needed them, the Venetians only offered him a refuge in their own city.

When word of the coup reached Venice she immediately awoke, shook herself, and marshalled all her energies to win back what she had lost. But the Genoese were not to be easily ousted. They kept up the strength of their garrison and prepared to defend their gains. The great trading empire that Venice had struggled so hard to win and secure during the thirteenth century seemed to be slipping from her grasp.

The Genoese struck with speed and secrecy forcing Venetian residents of Constantinople to flee.

A doge of Venice

Michael Paleologus, now crowned Emperor of Byzantium, rewarded his allies with a generosity that was truly remarkable. According to the terms of the Treaty of Ninfeo, published in 1261, Genoa was to be given the favored position formerly held by Venice. The grateful Emperor thus granted to the Ligurian Republic the sole ownership of streets and piers in Constantinople, immunity from tribute, and free passage for all her merchant ships. In addition, he bestowed on certain Genoese families who had been particularly friendly to his cause some commercially important real estate on the shores of the Black Sea as well as a number of key islands in the Aegean Sea.

The sudden loss of Constantinople should have jolted the Venetians. Their access to the terminal bazaars where traders haggled over silk and spices from the far places of the East was now lost. If they did not take steps to re-establish their contacts with the northern caravan routes—which were becoming more and more heavily traveled and which deposited the most sought-after goods in all of Europe on the shores of the Black Sea and the Aegean Sea—Venice's far-flung network of trade would almost certainly wither. With it would go not only her wealth, but also her prestige, her influence, and her political position in the world. Venice, however, had grown fat, and in growing fat had become complacent. She had held a monopoly position in the eastern trade for so long that she had begun to think that she could keep it without making any effort.

Now that the time had come for action, Venice found that she lacked both the muscle and the spirit to break Genoa's grip. For the next hundred years her efforts to wrest commercial control from Genoa were half-hearted.

Moreover, Genoa had decided that she ought to make her position in Constantinople more secure. This could be done by launching a series of assaults that slowly would whittle away the strength of the Venetian navy. Accordingly, she dispatched a sizable group of ships to carry out the first of such attacks. The task force was under a joint command; two men held the rank of Admiral—one a nobleman, Pierino Grimaldi, and the other, Perchelto Mallone, a commoner. This curious arrangement represented an attempt to reconcile conflicting elements always present within the city-state.

Early in the morning the fleet of thirty ships sailed out of the fog bank off the coast of Malvasia. They had not gone far when they came upon a Venetian fleet apparently much smaller.

"What sport!" Grimaldi exclaimed. "Fortune has delivered the Venetians into our hands. We shall sink them all. But we shall do it with style."

The Genoese closed in for the kill. The Venetians, taken by surprise, were thrown into utter confusion. There was time neither to deploy for combat nor to flee.

Then, with the Genoese only a few furlongs away, the course of events took a surprising turn. The leeward column of the attacking ships broke formation. Admiral Grimaldi's flagship, showing great discourtesy in the rules of seamanship, was passing under the stern of the Genoese vessel commanded by Admiral Mallone. As it came within hailing distance a furious Admiral Mallone cupped his hands and shouted, "Since you are so eager to attack, then attack. Show us poor commoners how a nobleman can fight."

A Venetian admiral

With that thrust, Mallone altered course and sailed away. To see his rival disgraced was more important to him than to rout the enemy. The pervading mistrust between commoner and nobleman had ruptured the command.

The Venetians waited, expecting some kind of trick. But Mallone's ships continued to sail off into the distance. And, as Grimaldi's fleet of thirteen ships, too deeply committed now to turn back, came within range, the Venetians fell upon it. In less than an hour nothing remained of Grimaldi's armada. The Admiral himself died at his post.

This could have been a turning point in history. If Venice had quickly followed up her advantage, she might have broken the back of Genoese sea power and regained her dominance in the eastern trade. But she didn't.

The years from 1290 onward witnessed an ever-growing truculence on the part of the Ligurian Republic. Having recovered from the effects of Admiral Mallone's retreat, the Genoese patched up the internal class strife that had ripped the city apart. Once again, the Genoese could present a solid front against the enemy.

Genoa, for the first time in the history of the two republics, began trading openly in the Adriatic, formerly considered the uncontested domain of Venice. Genoese ships began to prey on Venetian convoys with such success that they even threatened the stability of her coastal trade.

Considering the extremity of the threat, one might have expected the Venetians to mount a great counteroffensive. On the contrary, she seemed willing to venture no more than a series of inconsequential engagements not

A member of the Venetian Grand Council

unlike that of Malvasia. These encounters slowly drained away Venice's strength. Indeed, in one of them, the battle of Curzola, the Venetians lost all but one of her galleys. Although it could scarcely be known at the time, the outcome of the battle of Curzola was to have an important consequence, the effects of which would only be felt years later.

One of the Venetian ships was under the command of a certain Marco Polo. Marco had returned to his native city of Venice a year or so before after a long sojourn in China and other exotic lands of the Orient. The story goes that, turning up in rough Tartar sheepskins, he was first turned away as an impostor. He brought with him tales of fabulous lands, of incredible travels, and extra-

Marco Polo, traveler and soldier

Marco Polo, a prisoner in Genoa, tells of his journey to Cathay.

ordinary adventures. He also brought with him Chinese macaroni, which he introduced into Italy—and gunpowder. He had volunteered to outfit a ship and offer it under his own command in service to his country.

Marco's ship was sunk at Curzola. He himself was taken prisoner. Removed to Genoa, he was kept there in jail for many months. He had as a cellmate a popular writer of tales from Pisa, Rusticiana by name. Marco had nothing better to do than talk, and Rusticiana wrote down what he had to say. Within a year or so, the journal was published.

The Travels of Marco Polo excited the imagination of all Europeans—especially the Genoese. Marco was released from jail to find himself famous. In his journal he had drawn enticing pictures of the fabulous wealth to be found in the Indies. The citizens of Genoa, always adventurous, always imaginative, began to dream of finding a sea route to the wondrous land of Cathay, as China was then known, and the rich lands of the Indies. Marco Polo could scarcely have surmised that the very vividness of his account would be a factor in bringing about the decline of his native city.

After Curzola, while Venice rebuilt her navy, clashes at sea kept recurring. But no serious battle took place until 1350. Then, quite without provocation, a reckless young Genoese nobleman named Philip Doria sailed into the harbor of Negropont, located on the east Aegean coast of what is now Greece, and burned it down. Then, to cap the humiliation, he carried the keys of the city back to the Venetian trading island of Chios located five miles off the west coast of Asia Minor, where he hung them on the walls for all to see.

Here was an insult so outrageous that the Venetians could hardly allow it to pass unnoticed. The incident had a particular sting because Venice had long prided herself on having maintained a colony at Chios, which was ideally located to serve as a gateway to the silk and spice trades from the East. Venice showed again that, once sufficiently aroused, she was still able to act.

The Venetians evidently made up their minds to dispose of the Genoese as rivals once and for all. The city turned for assistance to the King of Aragon whose relations with them were friendly. Mounting a combined fleet of sixty-six ships, they set sail and encountered the Genoese navy at the mouth of the Bosporus. The engagement that followed is known as the battle of the Bosporus. It appeared that the outnumbered Genoese were about to be routed. But just as the battle was joined, a frightful storm arose. Ships ploughed into one another; or they were dashed against the rocks on shore. Neither adversary could withdraw. They fought on throughout the night.

When dawn came, the calmer sea, now gently rolling, revealed a carpet of corpses and broken timber. The flower of both navies had been lost to the unpredictable sea.

Only twelve ships remaining of the Venetian fleet limped back to the lagoons. Undaunted by her loss and fully confident of her power, Venice set about building a new fleet of one hundred vessels. But what she needed above all at this juncture was a leader to inspire her and crystallize her energies. There seemed to be no one on the horizon anywhere with the needed qualifications.

Yet, such a leader was about to appear.

The Fateful Hour

A few months later, Venice tasted revenge. A reconstituted fleet was placed under the command of a popular hero named Admiral Vettor Pisani. Pisani, himself the son of a distinguished Admiral, Niccolo Pisani, appealed to the Venetian imagination. Impulsive and hot-tempered, he was nevertheless a leader who knew how to inspire his men. Pisani sailed up the west coast into the Tyrrhenian Sea and soundly beat the Genoese. In fact, Pisani declared that if he had had a few more ships at his disposal, he would have sailed right into the harbor of Genoa itself.

But showing characteristic prudence, he turned away, sailed around the toe and heel of the Italian boot, and up the east coast as far as a town called Pola. There he went into winter quarters to repair his ships. He had not been there long when the Genoese navy, newly strengthened and enlarged, appeared in nearby waters.

Pisani wished to refrain from giving battle. His forces were weak. The plague had decimated Italy that winter, and many of his seamen had died. Others were still sick. His ships had been damaged in the fight in the Tyrrhenian Sea, and he had not yet been able to have them repaired.

He thought it would be bad judgment to go out and fight the Genoese.

However, the Grand Council had assigned two representatives ostensibly to advise Pisani, but really to spy on him. They overruled Pisani's protests and ordered him to challenge the Genoese vessels to battle. Pisani did not agree, but he was a sailor and accustomed to obeying orders. He reluctantly consented to carry the fight to the Genoese.

The latter, having the stronger force, were victorious. The result was a disaster for Venice. Pisani was lucky to escape with six vessels intact. When he reached Venice he was coldly received. The Grand Council, to avoid having any blame for the monumental defeat laid at their door, ordered Pisani thrown into prison. They then appointed Admiral Taddeo Giustiniani to replace him.

With their seapower broken and their admiral in jail, no substantial defence remained between Venice and the approaching Genoese navy. Panic gripped the city. Never, since the early days, had Venice been in such danger. Envoys were dispatched to the King of Hungary to make a treaty with him so that he would not throw in his lot with Genoa. But the king's terms were so insulting that Venice decided to reject them and take her chances. With Pisani in jail, there was only one man with the luster and ability to rally the flagging populace, but he was far away. His name was Carlo Zeno and he was busy harrassing the Genoese in the Levant. Messengers were dispatched to bring him home to meet the emergency.

A view of Venice

Protecting Venice and her lagoons from the open Adriatic was a chain of islands, some twelve in all. The southernmost—and largest—was Chioggia. Between the islands and the mainland a channel had been dredged 15 miles long to allow deep-water ships to reach the harbor. But the channel was a narrow one. Chioggia sat on the edge of it; whoever held Chioggia could rake the channel with cannon shot and flaming arrows—and for that reason could pose a threat to Venice herself.

On the morning of August 6, 1379, the Venetians' worst fears became a reality. Genoese ships were sighted off the outer islands. At this point the invading force didn't look too formidable to the Venetians, so the Council ordered Admiral Giustiniani to drive them off. His ships were moving to battle formation when the Venetians saw a sailor leap off a Genoese ship and start swimming toward them. Arrows hissed into the water all around him, but he managed to reach the Venetian ship where he was taken on board. He was a Venetian sailor who had been captured by the Genoese.

"It's a trap!" he warned, pointing across the water. "Don't go after them. A much larger force is waiting out of sight to overwhelm you."

The Venetians withdrew while there was still time.

But eleven days later, on the morning of August 17, the *Marangon,* greatest of San Marco's bells, began to ring as it had never rung before. Everyone recognized the sound of alarm. The citizens hurriedly gathered in the piazza before the great cathedral.

On one of the balconies, Doge Andrea Contarini, a smallish man of seventy years, moved into view. Only those standing near the entrance could see him clearly.

He had changed. The sparkle was gone from his eye.
Those expressive hands, once given to lively, excited
gestures, were hanging limp. Even his snow-white hair
had lost its luster. Andrea Contarini was tired. His
voice, however, was still strong.

"My countrymen, we have endured much. But now
the final blow has come. Last night at midnight we
received word that Chioggia has fallen." Slowly he raised
his thin right hand and pointed over their heads. "The
banner of St. Mark has been replaced by the Genoese
flag of St. George."

"You all know what this means," the Doge continued.
"Even if friendly ships tried to come to our rescue, the
Genoese would be able to drive them back easily. We
have no choice. As soon as possible, we will send an
emissary to Admiral Doria and at least ask him what his
terms for peace would be."

An audible groan went up from the assembled multi-

Contarini was re-
luctant to become
doge, but he remained
leader of Venice
through her darkest
hour.

tude. Abruptly the Doge withdrew into the cathedral.
He did not wait to face the scorn of his people.

The Genoese now held a dagger to the city's throat.
With the islands in their hands, they could easily shoot
their flaming arrows from the high wooden towers into
any ships trying to get into or out of the lagoon. On
shore, Genoa's allies, the citizens of Carrara and troops
from the King of Hungary, had effectively drawn a noose
around the city preventing any supplies from reaching
her by land.

Venice might have fallen an easy prey to assault if the
Genoese had chosen that moment to strike. But, reasoned
Admiral Doria, why risk a fight when Venice could be
starved into submission? He sat on his islands and
waited.

The populace, milling about and grumbling, were
convinced that they were already doomed unless Pisani
were set free to fight for them. He was the only one
who could hold off the Genoese until Carlo Zeno came
—that is, if he were ever coming.

Carlo Zeno was the subject of many heated discussions.
His name was on everyone's lips, even the Doge's. His
was the stuff of which heroes—and legends—are made.

When he was very young his parents had decided that
he should enter the priesthood. After all, such a vocation
was entirely appropriate for the son of a well-to-do
Venetian family. But young Carlo was by no means
temperamentally suited for such a rigorous and exacting
life.

A Venetian nobleman

At the age of nine he was sent to live as a clerk in
the household of the Pope at Avignon. When he was
only thirteen, he was returning home to Venice from

Avignon one day when he was set upon by robbers and beaten. Such was his spirit that he procured a pack of bloodhounds, hunted the robbers until he found them, and turned them over to the police. The robbers were promptly hanged.

He was next dispatched to the University of Padua. There he distinguished himself chiefly by the scrapes he managed to get into—and out of. Since this school was near Venice, he could continue his studies under his parents' watchful eyes. But the youth, then in his midteens, was not to acquiesce so quietly. Before long he had established himself as a colorful but reckless character.

He left the university and for five years wandered about as a mercenary soldier learning to lead men, planning and executing military strategy.

In time, he was drawn back to Venice. Upon his return, he became reconciled with his parents, who had long thought him dead. Next, he sought to be restored to favor in the Church. But the lack of activity did not suit him. Before long he was off to the wars, this time defending the Church of Christendom against the Turks. In spite of the nobility of his motives, the Church could not accept this breach of clerical piety. Subsequently, Carlo Zeno was again turned from the clergy.

Carlo traveled for several years as an ambassador for the King of Cyprus, but at length he decided to settle down. He married a girl who was not only surpassingly beautiful, but also rich, whom he had met while representing Cyprus. Subsequently his wife died, and Carlo Zeno, still young and handsome, wished only to go home again.

Once in Venice, according to his diary, he reflected, "In a maritime country, trade is of the highest utility, so I resolve to adopt the life of a merchant." He was barely thirty years old when he made up his mind to devote all his energies to business. Carlo invested wisely and traveled frequently to Constantinople. Soon his became the most familiar name in Venice. He was still young, a widower, and one of the richest merchants in the republic. He was also a dashingly romantic hero in an otherwise dreary time for the once proud city.

In the wake of the disaster at the battle of the Bosporus, when Venice had lost so many ships, the Doge pleaded with Carlo to come to the aid of the state. He was one of the few men left in the republic who might prevent Genoa from drumming Venice right out of the Mediterranean.

Carlo Zeno's varied career, his exploits in many fields, ranging from love to war to finance, all enhanced his appeal to his fellow citizens. This appeal was further glamorized by his demeanor and physical appearance, which was described by his grandson, the Bishop of Padua, as follows:

> Square-shouldered, broad-chested, solidly and strongly made, with large and speaking eyes, and a manly, great and full countenance; his stature neither short nor tall. Nothing was wanting to him which strength, health, decorum and gravity demanded.

In addition to his commanding presence, not the least of his gifts was his ability as an orator. It became a habit with him to give a ringing and stirring address to his

Venetians looked to Carlo Zeno, dashing young nobleman, to save the city from Genoese attack.

fighting men just before leading them into a battle.

Now Carlo Zeno was with his fleet in the waters off Constantinople, but he was urgently needed at home. The sun had long since set on the fateful day when Doge Contarini announced the fall of Chioggia. Contarini had dozed briefly during the evening. Now he was in his study awaiting the Genoese reply to his request for terms. His emissary, Signor Manzini, was shown into the high-ceilinged, oak-paneled room. The red curtains were closed. It was dark except for the corner in which the Doge sat. Candles illumined the small desk at which he read. The old man looked up. The expression on his visitor's face distressed him.

"Your face gives me their answer."

"It is hopeless, sir," the emissary nodded. "They know

we are at their mercy. It galls me to repeat the Admiral's words. 'Tell old Contarini this: Venice shall have no peace 'till we have bridled the bronze horses which stand upon the portico of your evangelist, San Marco.'"

"So," the Doge mused aloud, "they will accept no compromise. Well, we'll see."

"Do you think they will attack?" Manzini asked uneasily. He was tired. "Contarini, if they attack, what will we do?"

"Calm yourself, Signor. We'll just have to wait and see. Despair weakens your will. That is wrong, Manzini. If we are to survive, we must not lose the confidence of our people."

The next morning Doge Contarini stepped out onto his balcony to address the crowd that had assembled to hear the answer. He had slept. The weariness so evident yesterday was gone today. His voice had a new ring to it. He drew strength from his resolve.

The people listened to what he had to say. A dejected hush stole over them. But before they could panic, he gathered all his force and shouted, "Shall we quail before this threat? Shall we flee our beloved city, with all that it stands for? Shall we leave the achievements of our illustrious ancestors to a ruthless enemy? Picture, if you will, what will happen after we leave. Imagine the Genoese pushing and raging through your houses, plundering and destroying everything in their path."

He paused, waiting for this scene to take effect. Then he thundered on.

"Admiral Doria has done us a great service. He has reminded us how cowardly it would be for us to submit. No, never shall we allow the sons of Genoa to set foot

on the sacred soil of our city. The enemy shall not drive us from our homes. We will fight to the last drop of blood."

A mighty sound went up from the piazza. The crowd rocked to the rhythm of a chant: "We shall fight! We shall fight! We shall win! We shall win!"

Doge Contarini smiled as he fingered his rosary. That was what he wanted. The self-satisfied Venetians were now in a mood to sacrifice. That was what he had wanted all along—to induce in them a sacrificial mood, for the hour of their test was at hand.

This was no mean achievement for a man who, the day before, they had held in contempt.

In the piazzas, along the canals, artisans and clerks left their shops and workbenches and came forward to volunteer. High-born ladies paused before receptacles on street corners to strip themselves of their jewels and their

Doge Contarini harangues his people, urging them to stand fast.

Rich Venetians pledge jewels and valuables for the city's defense.

gold, letting rings and bracelets slide down their delicate fingers to clatter on top of others. The Grand Council's decree of an extra 5 percent tax on all transactions to receive funds was greeted with wholehearted enthusiasm. Fishermen and gondoliers clustered at the quays offering their vessels and themselves in the public service. The Grand Council announced that it would give ear to anyone who had a plan that would augment the defense of the city. Social distinctions vanished. Perhaps for the first time, Venetians stood elbow to elbow in a common cause.

It was the general populace who had to bear the greatest hardships. They gave tongue now to what was uppermost in their thoughts as with a single voice. They demanded that Vettor Pisani be released from prison and restored to his command as Admiral of the Navy. The members of the Grand Council could be stubborn no longer. They would heed the voice of the people.

On a sunny morning in the first week of October, the prison doors were thrown open and Pisani was set free. Haggard, thin, and pale from his time in prison, he was borne on the shoulders of the multitude to the Piazza of San Marco. At the sight of their hero, the crowd broke into cheers. They pushed and shoved to get close enough to touch him as he stood on a raised dais at Doge Contarini's side. The Doge raised his hand for silence.

Then before the huge gathering, in humility the Doge asked Pisani if he would wipe the indignities of the past from his memory and accept a return to his post as Admiral of the Venetian Navy. The crowd went wild. They shouted and cheered. It was Pisani now who asked for silence.

"My friends," he said, his voice unsteady with emotion, "you have never lost faith in me, and I for my part shall never lose faith in you. But the need now is for action. I must have sailors—men who are willing to die for

Vettor Pisani is released from jail to lead the fight against Genoa.

Venice. To those of you who are ready to serve in my navy I say, leave now. Go to your homes. Put your affairs in order. Then report to the arsenal for assignment."

Immediately the crowd began to disperse as Venetians hurried through the streets to their homes.

The response to Pisani's impassioned appeal was overwhelming. Within three days he had enough volunteers to man the numerous galleys—both new and reconditioned—that the arsenal had made ready for him.

But the citizens themselves faced a long and grinding trial. The Genoese ships still forbade access to the lagoon while her forces and those of her allies controlled the roads ashore. No food could find its way into the city. The women and old men stood aimlessly in the piazza waiting for some word. Children whimpered with hunger.

Fortunately for Venice, Admiral Doria still hesitated to attack the city. In Pisani's view, Doria's decision was the right one. Venice's will to resist was crumbling. The citizens weren't far from starvation. Pisani studied the situation for a long time. Finally, he saw that he had no choice. He would have to strike—to carry the battle to the enemy—if Venice were to be saved.

Pisani mustered his raw recruits—the clerks and artisans, painters, craftsmen, and accountants. They were for the most part men of peace; many of them had never been to sea. For the next six weeks, Pisani drilled them in basic seamanship. Then he rehearsed his plan in secret. He put them through their paces so often that the Grand Council began to think he was merely stalling for time.

Swords were offered to European kings in an effort to find Venice allies.

Admiral Vettor Pisani was a hero to Venetian citizens.

The longest night of the year came at last. This was the night on which Pisani had said he would strike. But the Grand Council did not really expect him to act.

Not long after sunset on the evening of December 21, the Venetian ships under the combined command of Contarini, Pisani, and Giustiniani sailed silently out under cover of darkness bound for the Genoese stronghold on Chioggia. Aboard one of the ships was Doge Contarini. He had insisted on serving in person.

When dawn came, the Genoese were startled to see a large flotilla of Venetian ships just off the shores of Chioggia. The Venetians put a large force ashore and advanced to the attack. Meanwhile, Pisani detached a smaller force of ships manned by seamen well rehearsed in his strategy. They sailed up to the mouth of Chioggia harbor and scuttled some barges, sinking them in the channel, and bottling up the bulk of the Genoese navy inside the harbor. On the beaches, the Venetians were being repulsed and driven back to their ships. But it didn't matter much. The diversion had enabled Pisani to carry out his strategic move.

Pisani did the same with the other two strategic entrances to the channel. Then he led his fleet into position on the seaward side of the island. There they would remain—where they could intercept ships coming to the aid of the Genoese. In one stroke the tables had been turned. Now the blockaders were blockaded. Now it was the Genoese who were threatened with starvation.

But how long could this cat-and-mouse game go on? The Venetians were feeling the pinch. The harbor, where vessels used to arrive almost every day, was as still as a graveyard. On the land side, all the roads by which the city customarily received food were blocked by Genoa's allies. Many a wealthy family had not so much as a loaf of bread on the table. Even the arsenal, source of Venice's strength and sinew, was shut down. The supply of timber for ship-building was exhausted.

Also, known to nobody but himself, Admiral Pisani was in a precarious situation. He could not promise what would happen to his small squadron if another Genoese flotilla, coming from afar, happened to show up off Chioggia. He would be caught in a crossfire. Furthermore, being on the seaward side of an island, he was at the mercy of winter storms. Should one arise, in no time his ships could be scattered and too badly knocked about to be capable of fighting.

Within Venice itself, weariness and hunger were eating away at the vitals of the populace. They had thought that their troubles would soon be over once Vettor Pisani was out of jail and in full command, with the city whole-heartedly behind him. But dreary day followed dreary day, and nothing changed.

And where was Carlo Zeno?

Contarini, who had returned to the Ducal Palace, was far from unmindful of the suffering of his people. But stubbornly, he refused to give up hope.

A delegation from the Grand Council waited on him and pleaded with him to surrender.

"Surrender?" he snarled, "Are you mad? Have we come this far only to give up now? It would be bad enough if the people were to come to me with this proposal. But you—the flower of the great noble families of Venice—where is your pride?"

At this point the Doge drew from its scabbard the ceremonial sword that hung at his side. "I swear upon this sword, I will die before I surrender." With that he placed both hands on the hilt of the sword, turned the point towards himself, and made ready as if to plunge it into his heart if they persisted.

"Wait," cried out the nobleman who had asked the question.

The Doge hesitated.

"Please, most honorable Doge. Put down your sword. You are our leader. We would be like lost children without you."

Contarini allowed himself to be swayed. Once again, he had silenced the voice of defeatism. But he knew he could not quiet the public clamor much longer. His repeated promise to produce Carlo Zeno was wearing thin. At last the day came when the Council refused to adjourn until the Doge had fixed a limit on the length of time he would ask his fellow citizens to hold out.

The Doge made up his mind. He turned and addressed the emissaries from the Grand Council.

"If Carlo Zeno has not arrived by the first day of the new year," he promised, "I will abandon the siege."

The new year was but four days away.

The Return of Carlo Zeno

Rumors reached Venice that Carlo Zeno was on his way. But there were also rumors that reinforcements were coming to help the Genoese. Pisani dispatched several of his small boats under command of Captain Penzano to be on the lookout and report.

Penzano stood on the bow of his ship peering into the damp, gray mist. His orders were clear. He was to abandon station and return to the mainland if nothing had changed by nightfall. He tried to keep such a possibility out of his mind. He needed all his powers of concentration if he were to see anything at all in this soupy atmosphere.

Suddenly the foretopman let out an excited cry: "Sails! Sails! I see sails to windward!"

Slowly Penzano turned his glass and swept the horizon. The lookout was right. There *were* sails. He could barely discern the shapes of them, not the colors. Whose vessels could they be?

"How many ships do you make out?"

"Can't tell, sir. Maybe four—maybe five."

Penzano swore. "They must be the vanguard of the Genoese flotilla," he muttered. "Where is Pisani? This is his command. If this is a trap, he is the one responsible for letting us into it."

Captain Penzano made up his mind in that instant he would not wait. If he gave the main body of the Genoese navy time to mass its strength against him, all would be lost. He determined to attack as soon as the ships came within range. His order ran down the line.

"Ships sighted on weather bow! When range closes to 1,000 yards—attack!"

Penzano had barely issued the order when the lookout again sang out, "Three more ships, Captain. That makes eight that I see now!"

Again the Captain cursed. Then he added quickly, "Belay that order. Change to 'stand by'!"

What else could he do? If any more phantom ships appeared in the fog, his fleet would be badly outnumbered. Ships were too dear to Venice to risk them recklessly against a stronger fleet. No, if any more ships were sighted he would not wait until tonight. He would abandon station now.

Penzano continued to ponder the alternatives. The wind picked up a bit, not much, but enough to blow off some of the fog.

"Fourteen," bellowed the lookout. "I can see fourteen, Captain."

Penzano spun in the direction of the clearing and fixed his glass on the ships. "My God," he muttered, "we'll never make it to the mainland. They'll tear us apart." He moved the glass over the ships again. Suddenly, through the mist, he caught a faint, familiar flutter of scarlet and gold. He shouted over his shoulder, "They're Venetian!" He paused a moment. Then he called in a tone of even greater excitement, "It's Carlo Zeno!"

Zeno's vessel paused at the line of Penzano's ships only

long enough to lower and raise his flag in salute. Then he sailed on fighting his way into Venice.

Women left their chores to welcome Carlo Zeno.

The entire town had turned out to welcome its savior.

Zeno's fleet had successfully weathered the hail of arrows rained upon it by the Genoese and, making its way down the long channel, had gained the security of the inner harbor. Now the crowd roared, "Long live Carlo Zeno!"

Zeno faced the people and saluted once again. He raised his arms in a dramatic gesture. There was a moment of utter silence. Then he shouted, "I have come."

He went on to explain why he had been delayed. Word had reached him near the Levant that he was urgently needed, and he had set sail at once for home. But as he was beating his way up the coast of Italy, he had encountered a huge Genoese sailing ship, the *Bichignona*, heavily armed and loaded with merchandise. The temptation was too great to resist. With his small galleys he had attacked her and won an overwhelming victory.

Venetian warships
entered harbor with
oarsmen at work.

Venice rejoiced. People poured through the streets, gathering in the piazza or on the Rialto in jubilant celebration, quite certain that their deliverance was at hand.

More was involved in Zeno's arrival than uplifting the spirits of the besieged. He had brought with him a cadre of experienced sailors to add to the ranks of desperate but inexperienced volunteers—the artisans and the men from the shops. But not knowing of the city's plight, he had brought little in the way of food beyond rations for his own men. The crisis for the city was far from ended.

Even as the people celebrated in the streets, within the Council Chamber of the great Ducal Palace, Zeno, Contarini, Pisani and other leaders sat discussing Venice's plight.

The Genoese, having had time to entrench themselves, were not going to be easily dislodged from Chioggia.

A messenger entered while they talked and handed a missive to Contarini. Here was news of a new threat and one that had to be dealt with at once. Stationed on a nearby island was quite a large band of mercenaries— soldiers from other lands who for pay fought for Venice. If the Genoese attacked the city, they were to come to the rescue as a fresh army of reserves. But idleness had made the professional soldiers restless. Some malcontents among them were hatching a revolt.

The Doge listened to the messenger, then ordered Carlo Zeno to go at once to placate the hirelings. Before the day was far advanced, Zeno had donned his armor, slipped out of the city, and was on his way to the island. He traveled with no more than a token escort consisting of six fighting men and two trumpeters.

The party stepped from the barge onto the land, the trumpeters announcing Zeno's arrival with an impressive flourish. Night was just closing in. The mercenaries came running and shouting from every direction. Zeno marched straight through their ranks to the campfire. He stood for a moment without uttering a word. The firelight glistened on his breast plate. Dancing shadows accentuated the lines of determination on his face.

One of the men who was with him described the scene afterwards. "His presence so stilled the commotion that the storm seemed in one moment to turn to calm."

Zeno proceeded to address the mercenaries in terms they could understand: "Soldiers, have you come here to fight against Venice? No, you have come for the reward of driving Genoa from these shores. But what holds you back then? Money? Did you think that Venice would be unwilling to pay you? Such a thought insults a proud state, and it insults me as a Venetian. I personally will guarantee to pay you from my own coffers, I who am giving service to noble Venice without pay."

Zeno's six guardsmen stepped forward. With one gesture each drew forth a purse that he had concealed beneath his tunic. They threw the gold at the feet of the *condottieri,* as the mercenaries were called. "Here are five hundred ducats," said Zeno. "When we have won, the republic will pay you another five hundred. Now, let us hear no more about money. If you doubt my word, draw your swords and step forward. To test my honor will be your final act."

The money, the boast, and the insult combined with the pomp were all perfectly calculated to impress the mercenaries. From that time on, they were Carlo's to command.

For the next several months the combined fleets of Pisani and Zeno kept the Genoese bottled up. There were uneasy moments, to be sure. One of them came when the city-state of Carrara, an ally of the Genoese, sent out a full squadron to aid the beleaguered garrison on Chioggia. But Zeno attacked with his ships while Pisani prevented the Genoese from going to their rescue. In the end they were driven off.

Such skirmishes continued until the early months of spring. By that time, the Genoese found themselves entirely out of food. They were reduced to eating rats and mice. When the rodents were gone, the besieged had nothing to live on but a kind of bouillon made by boiling shoe leather in fresh water. Their men were too

weak to give battle. Many were already dying of starvation. They could not hold out much longer.

Carlo Zeno was
wounded at Chioggia.

In one heavy attack on Chioggia in April, the Venetians
bombarded the islands with cannon. Their shots went
wild, but one salvo hit a tower in Chioggia. Admiral
Doria was killed by the falling bricks. Napoleone Grimaldi succeeded Doria in command of the Genoese navy.
Immediately, he sent his deputies to wait on the Doge.
Carlo Cangiamini, the chief emissary, petitioned Contarini as follows: "We have fought fairly; we have ob-
served the laws of God and man. We yield to hunger,
not to arms. As fellow Christians we expect that you
will honor our request to sail from Chioggia unmolested."

One can imagine the Doge's feelings. He could hardly
forget the fear and deprivation that was being visited on
his own city. But most of all, he did not forget the
message that his emissary Manzini had brought from the

Genoese when the Venetians sued for peace. The words
still echoed in his ears: "Tell old Contarini this: 'Venice
shall have no peace' till we have bridled the bronze horses
which stand upon the porch of your evangelist, San
Marco.'"

For some minutes the Doge pondered silently the
sudden turning of the tables. Then he addressed himself
to the waiting Cangiamini:

"As fellow Christians you expect that we will allow
you to sail freely out of Chioggia. Tell me, Signor, where

The victory over the Genoese at Chioggia was celebrated with pomp by the Venetians.

was your 'Christian' attitude last fall when we asked for peace? Why should we let you go, you who have threatened to burn our city to the ground? Go back to Grimaldi, and tell him that we are still waiting for him to bridle the bronze horses which stand upon the porch of San Marco."

"Is that your final answer, Doge Contarini?"

"Yes."

When Cangiamini related the Doge's answer to Grimaldi, the Admiral grew pale. The latter, once a large

Weary Genoese prisoners receive help from the ladies of Venice.

man but now thin and wan from his starvation diet, could hardly restrain his feelings.

"How could this happen to us?" he cried. "Only six months ago we had the Venetians right at the edge of submission."

"It is that, Contarini; he has beaten us. He kept their spirit alive until help could come. Now we, the besiegers, are trapped by Carlo Zeno. Oh, that the sea might open and swallow him up!"

"We can hold out no longer," sighed the Admiral. "Call the captains together. I will meet with them here aboard *La Bella* and advise them of the Doge's answer. We must decide what to do."

The meeting was short, for despair had sapped their will to resist. Word was sent to Contarini that the Genoese would surrender unconditionally. The Venetians quickly mustered dozens of barges to pick up their worn and weary enemy.

In Venice a great holiday spirit filled the air. Gathering in the Piazza of San Marco, all along the canals, the citizens chattered excitedly. The Genoese prisoners were being brought ashore.

The treaty bringing peace between Venice and Genoa was signed in August, 1381. By that time the quays along the canals were stacked high with the goods of many nations. Never again would Venice have reason to fear her hated rival, Genoa.

The Passing of an Era

Venice now entered on a hundred years of the greatest prosperity she had ever known. It was a period of splendor and magnificence far surpassing anything her citizens had enjoyed before.

It was the age when some of the greatest painters of the Renaissance captured the floating spirit of Venice in her heyday. The art critic Bernhard Berenson has said that the Venetians excelled in painting the special values of the Renaissance, "delight in life with the consequent love of health, beauty and joy." They painted magnificent processions, Berenson noted, which satisfied the Venetian's love of his state and his love of splendor.

Many great names in art among their ranks—the Bellini brothers, Carpaccio, Titian, Tintoretto. Their works hung in public places, mostly in the ducal Palace, a constant reminder to Venetians of their city's achievements. The glass-making and leather-working crafts flourished as well. More ornate and spectacular palaces arose along the banks of the canals, adorned inside and out with splendid treasures brought back from the far corners of the known world.

The private lives of her citizens too, were marked by elegance and extravagance. Great feasts were the order

Giovanni Bellini's *Madonna and Child* is but one masterpiece from Venice.

of the day. Masked balls began at midnight and went on until the next noon. One Venetian host, to impress a roomful of guests from uncouth Europe, served them on plates of solid gold. Then, when the banquet was ended, he ordered the servants to sail the plates out the window and into the lagoon. Venice was a name uttered with both admiration and envy everywhere in the civilized world.

But the music of her costume balls, drumming in Venetian ears, drowned out the alarms of approaching doom.

Her citizens changed. With an excess of wealth, they had less zeal. They were no longer so interested in going to sea, in searching out merchants of other lands, in undertaking all the adventurous enterprises necessary to acquiring wealth; they were more interested in spending it.

As a city, Venice altered her policy toward her neighbors. Interested now in extending her borders over the plains of northern Italy, she became involved in a quarrel with the nearby city-state of Milan, a feud that sapped much of her strength and vitality. This was a new course, one never before taken in her history.

Still another threat loomed in the East. The forces of Islam, spearheaded by the Turks, drove northward to the very borders of the old Byzantine Empire. Wherever they went in the Levant, they ousted European traders from the favored positions that they had enjoyed since the Crusades. The Turks were rapidly approaching Constantinople, the last great stronghold barring the onrush of the infidels to the west.

Terrified that she was about to lose that source of trade, Venetian diplomats sought audiences with all the powerful princes of the West, exhorting them in the name of Christendom to send their armies to stop the Turks from coming any further.

But the western leaders regarded Venice's pleas with amused indifference. They had not forgotten how Venice in the past had made private deals with the Turks when such arrangements had been to her commercial advantage.

Now Venice had reason to regret the plunder of Constantinople. The attack had left that citadel so weakened that it could not hold out long. The Turks occupied the city in 1453.

The Queen of the Adriatic, however, was about to suffer an even heavier blow. In the year 1495, Venice was buzzing with news—but it was news filled with foreboding. Ever since Marco Polo had returned from Cathay with his tales of fabulous riches, men had dreamed of finding another route to the East. Now came word that the Portuguese explorer Bartolomeo Diaz had indeed found one around the Cape of Good Hope at the southern tip of Africa. He had returned with fabulous stories of the trade winds that would blow a sailing ship all across the Indian Ocean—and then, if the ship waited six months, would blow her all the way back again.

The implications of this discovery were monumental —and plain at once to every seagoing Venetian. It meant that Venice had lost her strategic position astride the trade routes of the world.

The situation worked out something like this: At every point along the route from the East, wherever goods were transported, wherever they changed hands, wherever they were broken out of bulk, somebody made a profit. Now they could travel by water, in bulk all the way, from ports in the Indies or China or Arabia to market in London, Bruges, or the Hanseatic ports on the North Sea.

Venice's trade did not stop all at once. But the handwriting was on the wall. And another factor further dimmed the importance of Venice's position. Great nations were arising all over Europe, swallowing up the smaller political bodies, engulfing whole large areas under one rule. The importance of the city-state was reaching its end.

And what of that other contending power? Genoa recovered somewhat while Venice was busy feuding with

Milan. But she was never able to regain her eminence as a trading power in the Mediterranean. Her citizens as individuals, however, retained their venturesome spirit. Their enterprise took two directions. The less hardy but more financially oriented Genoese continued to solidify the Bank of St. George as one of the most respected commercial institutions of Europe. Later her banking interests would give Genoa's businessmen a dominant role in Spain's economic life. In fact, Genoa indirectly provided much of the backing for Columbus' first voyage.

Other more physically adventurous Genoese continued to look seaward and dream great dreams. The bolder among them picked up and moved on to Portugal. There, under the stimulating and imaginative guidance of Henry the Navigator, they found an outlet for their seafaring genius. The post of Admiralty of the Portuguese Navy remained in the hands of members of the Pessagni family of Genoese origin from 1317 until 1448. From this position of influence the Pessagnis were able to provide positions of opportunity for many of their former countrymen. It was the Genoese who not only taught navigation to many of the Portuguese, but also fired their imaginations with tales of the fabulous riches to be had from the Indies. And where had they come by these tales? From the lips of a Venetian—Marco Polo.

Was it such accounts that excited Christopher Columbus a century-and-a-half later and prompted him to set out to try to find a new way to the eastern world?

For both rivals, the great period of their prosperity had ended. But each, in its altogether different and characteristic way, left its imprint on posterity. Genoa opened up much of the world through her explorers, her adventurers, her navigators, and through her bankers. Venice, through the magnificence and opulence of her treasures, of her culture, made lasting contributions to art and to letters. These, plus her spirit and the loveliness of her setting, have left to succeeding generations a shrine where visitors go and will continue to go to gaze upon her beauty and refresh and renew themselves.

Portuguese ships sailed with Genoese navigators.

BIBLIOGRAPHY

Genoa: How the Republic Rose and Fell by J. Theodore
Bent. London: C. K. Paul & Co. 1881.

Venice: An Historical Sketch of the Republic by Ho-
ratio F. Brown. London: Rivington, Percival & Co.
1905.

Gleanings from Venetian History by Frances Marion
Crawford-London. London: Macmillan and Co.,
Ltd. 1907.

*The Venetian Republic: Its Rise, Its Growth, and Its Fall
421–1797* by W. Carew Hazlitt. London: A. and C.
Black. 1900.

The Pageant of Venice by Edward Hutton. London:
John Lane. 1922.

The Story of Venice by Thomas Okey. New York: E. P.
Dutton & Co., Inc. 1931.

The Makers of Venice by Mrs. Margaret Oliphant. London: Macmillan and Co., Ltd. 1898.

PICTURE CREDITS

INDEX

ABOUT THE AUTHOR
AND
CONSULTING EDITOR

M. GREGG ROBINSON became interested in the seesaw struggle between Venice and Genoa to dominate Mediterranean trade while still at Bowdoin College. He pursued his interests while securing his Master's degree in English at Boston University.

A charter boat captain, Mr. Robinson has also taught English at Bentley College. He now lives in Buzzards Bay, Massachusetts, and operates a boat yard.

EDWARD R. SAMMIS, Consulting Editor of the Trade Routes Series, is the author of many newspaper and magazine articles. During World World II, he was chief of the worldwide feature service of the Office of War Information. He now devotes his time to writing and editing books.